Creatively HOMELESS

How to escape debt and travel the world

David and Laura Helen

FOREVER FAMILY
FOREVER FREE

WARNING – DISCLAIMER

BOOKS BOOST BUSINESS

Books Boost Business is part of the Forever Family Forever Free group of companies whose address can be found at booksboostbusiness.com.

This book was created using the ***"We Coach Your Story"*** *service at BooksBoostBusiness.com This is the simplest service that we offer. We have a one-to-one coaching session with you, where we help you release the content from your heart and pour it onto the page. We also provide 3 different cover designs for you to choose from, and then create your final cover.*

We do the typing, editing and publishing for you.
From an Idea to a published book.

First Edition
First published in the UK 2020 – David & Laura Helen
www.booksboostbusiness.com
Book: Creatively Homeless – David & Laura Helen
ISBN-13 **978-1-913501-56-3**
laurahelen@foreverfamilyforeverfree.com

BOOKS BOOST BUSINESS

WHAT IS THE BOX

We often refer to ourselves as living outside the box!
But what do we really mean by this?
I am going to use a short explanation I once heard at a Tony Robbins seminar as it is funny and makes the point we are trying to portray.

> ***The average person grows up in their box home, in their box room, they get packed off to their box school enjoying their box lunch, with kids in the same boxes as them, same age and ability. Years later they graduate and rather than break free, they go out and a buy a box home of their own. Every day, they wake up in their box home, hop into their box car and drive to their box office where they work on their box screen. They drive home in their box car, return to their box home, sit in front of the box to enjoy their box dinner. If they are feeling a little wild, they will go into the kitchen into their box fridge and pull out a cylinder to change state and relax!***

Now this is a little extreme and cheeky, but it really makes you think. The majority of people are in a system, in a fixed routine. Take the kids to school, go to work, pick the kids up, feed them, get them to bed, watch tv... same again tomorrow... all the while living just over broke whilst trying to maintain an image they feel the need project to look successful and get approval. But constantly trying to 'keep up with Jones's is making them struggle even more.

Too many are linking success to the social conditioning they have received. They must have the house, the car, the kids, the income.... Without the art of fulfilment, life is empty, mundane and unsatisfying. Many people wake up mid-life and think, WOW how did I get here? Is this my life? They start to try new things and take new risks; they often try to *buy* themselves happy. We refer to this as their mid-life crisis! For a moment, they woke up! They broke out of the system, they got to see outside of their routine. They suddenly realised they are not fulfilled; they are not happy and living life to their full potential. Too many get called out as a mid-life crisis and fall back into their routine, others change their lives forever. Unfortunately, many people only wake when a tragedy happens, either they get really ill or they lose someone close to them. This shocks them so much they re-evaluate their lives. Do not wait for bad news to shock you into making changes – start creating your life your way, now!

FOREWORD

Life shapes us. Our past moulds us. Positively. Negatively.

You know when you meet someone along your day and you're like, who IS this person?!

Welcome to Laura. She came into my world, our network like a firework. All the flash bang wallop of a rocket and a wonderful spark of life, energy and contagious enthusiasm to help, support others and to make a positive impact, a positive difference.

Get beyond the surface, I started to learn about Laura's unique lifestyle. I was not surprised to discover she had had so many adventures, all generated by an appetite to live, positively. To live positively is weaved throughout her DNA, and as such she never settled in one place for too long, yet completely settled in who she is, was and will be.

She has a zest for life that is infectious, and I am thrilled to see she has put her journey into words to help others live their same kind of unique life. Look, I'm a motivational speaker. One thing I realised over many years is that success is defined by contentment, adventure and life lived, not money spent.

When success comes at the cost of health, sick-cess, you've just lost.

So many people I know who have 'success', lack the very thing Laura has, contentment.

That's true success and by following the lessons and teachings within this book, maybe they could recognise that life is for living, money is for earning, then spending, the world is to travel and home is where you are.

Always make where you are, where you want to be.

Ultimately, it's the adventures, family and memories that really matter.

So, read this book, enjoy it and learn from the lessons Laura and her family share. Work-life balance is a myth, but you CAN find a way to live life to the full so that at the end of your days, you have a heart full of memories, not a heart full of regrets.

Live. Positively.

Brad Burton
The UK's #1 Motivational Business Speaker
BradBurton.biz

ENDORSEMENTS

What others are saying...

"My mind is officially blown away!
I had a power hour with Laura and I have more certainty than ever! If you want to feel liberated (even if you think you already are), free to live the life of your dreams (even if you think you already are doing it), speaking to Laura is a MUST! She will definitely help you to destroy and demolish ANY of your doubts and second-guessing. And by the way, I am not that kind of person who is second-guessing often!
Thank you, Laura, for helping me with my wobble, I am so happy I reached out!
p.s. everyone else – yeah, thank me later for the recommendation, I know you WILL LOVE LAURA! "

Olga Geidane
Motivational speaker and Mindset Coach

"Laura is a loving mother, she allows her children to be authentically themselves. Schooling through life skills and experiences, she has chosen to learn through being.
Education in schools is a thing of the past for Laura as she travels the world with her family growing and becoming.
Her children are authors and share to audiences their insights.
Positive energy and love are abundant in everything she does in life.

Amanda Hill Ryall
Conscious Parent Coach & Podcaster

"Laura inspires me, she has created a life the way she wants to with her family and she gets to do what she loves. That is extraordinary and that inspires me. Laura, thank you for being who you are!"

Anna Garcia – Relationships Intensive

"My life changed quickly after connecting with Laura, she has had fantastic professionalism, kept calm during phases of extreme pressure. Her content has not only helped me but also others as I have witnessed her put other people at ease under times of stress and empower them to steer their lives in the direction they want!

I would recommend Laura to anyone serious about taking action to change their life when they don't know where or how to start."

Kealan Harrington – Going the Ultra Mile

"A huge, big thank you to Laura & David, they have been amazing, absolutely amazing, I love them. Laura has a way of making you face your fears, she is very direct and it's tough love, but it's all in a good way. You can feel her looking into your heart when she is helping you. That is the key part, she does want to help, and she does help, she is fantastic and worth every single investment opportunity, whatever you want to do, to get on with your book. I call Laura a force of nature because she has had a massive influence on me, this is with respect and thank you..."

Martin Upton
Anorexic Healer Project

"Laura you are an amazing person! I got to know you on a personal level which was amazing, I just want to say you are definitely an entrepreneur, you have a beautiful heart and a beautiful mind, you have created a family that strive to become better, mentally, physically, emotionally and spiritually. I thank you for being a friend to me, thank you so much Laura. I appreciate everything you have done. Continue to change the world, continue to believe in what you believe in because you are on the right path..."

Karim Ramos
Realtor Associate at RE/MAX

This isn't just a book it's a 'how to' guide to create a real action plan.

Each chapter has an activity, and these activities stack up on each other to help you create an action plan to redesign your life on purpose. Really jump all in with these activities, going over each to give you a clear understanding of what, how, where and why you want to achieve your dream life.

We have made this interactive with an online video and cheat sheet program that you can go through at your own pace.

You can check out *All the Activities* here.

"When would NOW be a great time to design your Destiny"

Activities.foreverfamilyforeverfree.com/destiny

Contents

WHO IS THE BOOK FOR

When we started this book, it would probably have appealed a lot more to people who were already working at home or who already had their own businesses and were making money online. But since the crazy pandemic years we've just gone through, more and more people, and more and more employees, have realised that they can do what they need to do from the comforts of their own home. And if they can do it from home, doesn't this mean they can do it anywhere with an internet connection?

You have overcome so much whilst going through the craziness that has been the pandemic. It was challenging. It was tough. It was scary. But you managed to homeschool and have fun and bond with your children.

It was challenging to have them at home and still commit to your work placement and your job. But you managed to do that too. Maybe you even did better than you did in the office.

While the pandemic brought fear and closed many doors, it also brought opportunities and opened up many other new doors.

We discovered the power of virtual meetings, virtual get-togethers with family and friends, virtual schooling, even virtual activities and after school clubs for our kids.

Think how much time you used to spend commuting, sat in traffic or on the same hour-long train ride every single day, and chauffeuring your kids around.

People think that they can't be as productive at home as they can at the office. But by simply removing all your commuting time, you have so much more usable time that you could spend doing something you love or being super productive in your virtual workplace or in your virtual school.

Our minds have been opened to new possibilities.

If all you need is the internet and each other, what is stopping you from taking a leap of faith and creating a life of freedom and adventure?

Maybe it's knowing where to start.

This book is for people who want to travel, who want a different life, who want to try a different way of doing things, but who don't know what is out there.

You may have seen travel bloggers all over your social media. They seem to travel the world, living in luxury. If only you had millions to do the same. If only you had this huge following. If only you had millions or even thousands in the bank. If only you knew how they travelled and made money. If only you knew their secrets. If only.

But what if you looked at it differently. What if you knew how a family started travelling while in tens of thousands of pounds of debt, with no money behind them, no backup plan, no plan B, no safety net. Yet, they've travelled the world for six years now, creating life on their own terms, and exploring the world, and its different cultures and languages. Whilst doing this, they've managed to also pay off their debts, get out of that chokehold of owing money and start to build their very own bank, whilst world schooling and having travel adventures with their children. This is our story. It could be yours too.

Who is this book for?

In this book, we will take you step by step through the process of creating a plan to help you and your family achieve the lifestyle you want. We'll tell you how we travelled our way out of debt and into a life of freedom, connection and fun. We'll teach you the lessons we learnt (usually the hard way), so that you can avoid making the mistakes we made.

In each chapter, you will find an activity and resources to take you one step closer to your goal.

This is not just a book of ra, ra, ra, yeah, yeah, you could have it all. We want to help you take action, so you can start your new journey now and start making a difference.

This is the book we wished we'd had when we first started out.

So let's dive in and get started.

You can check out *is this book for you* here.

"When would NOW be a great time to make a decision?"

Activities.foreverfamilyforeverfree.com/destiny

Part 1:

Designing Your Dream Lifestyle

CHAPTER 1

Understanding Your Why

Why we help people create a life they love

The reason why we are really driven to help more people live like we do is because we have so many friends and family and acquaintances who we love who work so hard. They're stuck in that rat race. Fifty weeks of the year, they work so hard. They're not particularly happy. They're doing it just to pay the bills. They call a job, "Just Over Broke", and then for two weeks of the year, they get to go on holiday and they get to live how they'd love to live. They have the most incredible two weeks ever. And even though they might think that they're being fake – "This is too fancy, we could never afford to live like this" – they're being their true selves. They're actually happy.

Now, imagine if every day was a holiday. Imagine you have two weeks where you go off to work, rather than 50. This is how we look at life and this is how our life has turned around. When the world is open, and as it should be, we go to self-development events. We go to networking events. We speak on stages. We go and participate. That is work to us.

So when we laugh and joke about the 50 weeks compared to the two weeks, we literally do the opposite. We'll have five days here, three days there, seven days here, where we go away and we work non-stop. We are there before the event opens. We are there until after it closes. We put our all into networking, making a difference, growing and expanding our network, and improving our business and ourselves. The other 50 weeks, we get to play, explore, have adventures and serve our clients with the best of what we can offer.

Our original why was to get ourselves out of debt and to create a life where we both get to spend lots of quality time with our kids, watching them grow up, learn, discover, and explore the world together.

Now six years on, our why is still to spend as much time creating magical moments with our children before it gets uncool for cuddles. This time the money we are saving from not having to pay bills can be used for our nest egg, compounding away and earning us passive income. We are all learning and growing together, in life and in business. We are very much heart centred, focusing on how we can add massive value and serve others as best we can, whilst creating passive income that will support ourselves and our children in the future. Our vision is to create a sustainable island and financial abundance for our children, so they have many more choices when it comes to choosing how they will live their best lives.

You can check out *Understanding your why* here.

You need a why so strong that it pulls you through the tough days. If you get this right, you will succeed! You will only fail if you quit trying!

Activities.foreverfamilyforeverfree.com/destiny

CHAPTER 2

Understand Your Numbers

Now, not everyone reading this book will be in debt. Some people may be okay financially. They might not have masses of money, but they might have some savings. Whatever your circumstances, you still need to know your numbers. You need to know what your life costs each month right now, how much you have left at the end of each month, and what savings you have before you can start making a plan.

To make it as easy as possible, download our 'Know Your Numbers' worksheet, fill in the numbers where prompted and it will do the maths for you. It may even suggest a few things that you hadn't thought of. It will definitely help you get super clear on what your numbers really are. When you know exactly where you are, it's much easier to find your way out of debt, if that is your circumstance, and move forward.

Before you get started, you will need to get your last three months' bank statements, so that you can find out where you are spending your money.

It may take you a couple hours to actually complete the work sheet, to find out all your numbers, what you spend and where you spend it. But I would definitely recommend that you do this.

When we finally did this and put it all together, we knew exactly where we were. We could then see what our outgoings were monthly, right there, in black and white.

When you start adding everything together, your monthly outgoings may be much bigger than you realised.

Then when you start comparing your wages to your outgoings, you may think, "Oh my goodness, we have so much month left at the end of our paycheck." At least, that's how it was for us.

FIRST, WE REDUCED OUR EXPENSES AS MUCH AS POSSIBLE

- TV LICENCE
- USING ENERGY LIGHT BULBS
- HARDLY USING THE ELECTRIC HEATERS
- CHOPPING DOWN OUR OWN FIRE WOOD
- STOPPING GYM MEMBERSHIP
- STOPPING NETFLIX
- STOPPING AMAZON PRIME
- RUNNING ONE CAR
- EATING BUDGET FOOD
- NOT EATING OUT
- NO TREATS – CIMEMA / THEATRE / BOWLING / ETC

So the options are to reduce your outgoings or increase your income.

We had already reduced our outgoings to the minimum – there was no wiggle room. So we had to find a place where it would cost us less to live.

Some people thought we were crazy to give up our jobs and fly off into the world and do the crazy things we did.

But one of our first destinations, Costa Rica, cost us just $300 a month, plus maybe $100 to feed four of us for the month, and that included eating out. The cost of living there was so different compared to our monthly outgoings in the UK. I think it was less than a quarter of we were previously paying.

So rather than panicking, how am I going to replace my high-paying job, you need to think how much you will need to earn to create this incredible lifestyle you want.

It was not hard for us to make $400 a month to cover our costs in Costa Rica.

When you can get your outgoings very low, you can see that you don't need to work very hard to make enough money, or you can keep working at that faster pace and pay back any debt or save quicker. You just need to turn things on their head. Look at things from outside the box and break those boxes open.

It is so important to know where you really are financially. It's important to get real about your finances and not just paint a pretty picture that helps you get through each day. It's also important to be truthful and not believe the crazy, deep, dark story you may have been telling yourself about how bad things are. You need to know the truth, where you really are.

It is very common for people to not actually know their true numbers, i.e. what they have coming in and going out, what savings they have available, how much debt they actually have or how much spare income they actually have. It's very easy to bury your head in the sand. Some people pretend everything's all right. Meanwhile, they are absolutely drowning and aren't sure how to get their way out of debt. Some people know they're in a little bit of trouble, but are full of doom and gloom. They make it so much worse and so much darker than it actually is. Some people are so much closer to freedom than they could ever really imagine.

So knowing your numbers really is crucial. It will help you to choose a strategy that suits you best. It is a really simple and easy thing to do, but very few people actually write down all the figures and work out exactly where they are financially.

ARE YOU ONE OF THOSE PEOPLE OR ARE YOU GOING TO **TAKE ACTION?**

You can check out *Know your Numbers* here.

Only when you know your real numbers, can make a real plan!

Activities.foreverfamilyforeverfree.com/destiny

CHAPTER 3

Could You Live For Less?

Once you know your numbers, you can start looking at where in the world you could afford to live for less.

We would recommend going on dreamy sites such as Airbnb and having fun searching for different places to live. You can do this as a family activity.

Our trip to Central America cost us $300 a month for four of us to live in Costa Rica. Our only bills were food. And there were so many beautiful trees and fruits around us. So our food costs were minimal.

And we had a pool and we were by the beach, and we were in nature and we were learning Spanish. And we were exploring with the locals. That was truly priceless, but that $300 was nothing, compared to what we were paying for our home, council tax, water, gas, electricity, our car, tax, the MOT, the repairs every month, in the UK.

Then do a search and discover where in the world you could live at half the cost, because with Airbnb, everything's included, apart from your food. And if the accommodation is crazy cheap, I can almost guarantee that the food and cost of living are really cheap too.

You can confirm the cost of living in each country on the world data website and you can even narrow your search down further to specific towns and cities. This cost of living data includes food, and the main essentials, including haircuts and clothes.

- https://www.worlddata.info/cost-of-living
- https://www.numbeo.com/cost-of-living

The world is an amazing place to discover. We've been taught how to do things, how to live in our box house and go to our box office. We spend all our time in our box office trying to pay for the box house that we're never in.

When you look at the world differently, you can discover new possibilities. On Airbnb, you can find out where you could live for months for a certain budget, even half your normal budget. Just allow yourself to dream and realise you could pay everything off in half the time by living somewhere wonderful or even working half the amount of time.

You could have the time and energy to build those bonds, mend those relationships, and have strength in your relationships and in your family that you've never had before. You can spend real quality time together, exploring the world, having adventures, smiling, laughing and loving together.

So now that you've looked on Airbnb, write down in the space below some of your favourite destinations and the monthly cost for you and your family to live there. Just by writing it down, a dream becomes a goal. We'll show you throughout the rest of the book how to achieve it, how to make it happen and how to turn that goal into your living reality, and even how to travel your way out of debt.

Could You Live For Less?

My favourite places	How much it will cost to live there for three months

Activity Live for Less

1. Visit the Airbnb website: Airbnb.com or Airbnb.co.uk
2. Don't enter a specific place, just enter one to three months.
3. Enter the number of people who will be staying.
4. Adjust the price down below your number, or even half the number you are paying right now to live

You can check out *Live for Less* here.

Watch the guided video and extras that we share when we search for places

Activities.foreverfamilyforeverfree.com/destiny

CHAPTER 4

Security, Certainty And Sustainability

To create your life by design a big part of that will be creating a sustainable income remotely. You will need to have steady and reliable sources of income. This will give you more choices and more freedom. This may take time and need tweaking and changing as you learn and grow but it is most definitely worth the time to get it right.

Make money while you sleep

One thing we learnt early on was to turn our earned income into passive income. We learnt this from Robert Kiyosaki, the author of *Rich Dad Poor Dad*. Earned income is where you exchange your time for money. This means that the amount you can earn is limited by the number of hours you work, whether you work 8, 10, 12 or 16 hours a day.

Passive income is where you work once, and get paid time and time again. When you create a system where you can get paid while you're not working, or paid while you sleep, that is when you can make a big difference to your income.

Have multiple sources of income

Having multiple sources of income is much more secure than relying on just one. With a job, you have one source of income (or two if you have a second job). If you work for yourself and have 10 clients, you have 10 sources of income. So even if a couple of clients drop off, you still have eight sources of income.

If you manage to write a book, you can sell many books, each giving you a small royalty. Say you sell 10 books a day and earn a royalty of £3 per book, that's an income of £210 a week (10 x £3 x 7). When you write a book, you work once, and get paid time and time again.

You could also create a digital product such as online coaching or 'how to' videos that get your clients from A to B, and then sell them for £37, £99 or even £250. You don't need to sell many of them to cover your living and travelling expenses.

- £37 x 5 a day x 7 days = £1,295 per week
- £99 x 2 a day x 7 days = £1,386 per week
- £250 x 1 a day x 7 days = £1,750 per week

I'm sure most of you don't need an income of £1,295 each week, we sure don't, but it is achievable.

David used to trade nine hours of his life a day for his income. We used some of that income to create our digital products, investing in graphic designers, video editors, website coders and marketing, etc. Now we are creating more income from our digital products than David earned in his day job, and you can do the same.

We go into more detail about how to earn an income online in the next chapter.

Passive income from savings

The next step is to turn your passive income (your digital products income) into your very own money machine. We use the power of compound interest where we currently earn 1% a day (you can find more info in the Resources section at the back of the book) and time to give us an even bigger return on our investment, which means a bigger sum to retire on, and the peace of mind and sense of security that goes with that. So even if the technology changes, or your competitors come out with a better product, or you just don't want to sell anymore, you still have passive income coming in from your money machine, all the time earning interest on top of interest on top of interest.

Live within your means

By staying in places with a low cost of living, house sitting for free and shopping and eating locally, we can live comfortably without spending a lot of money.

This is how we managed to pay back extreme amounts of debt. We still do that now, even though we are debt free. We have a nest egg, we have our investment accounts, and we have our high-interest savings accounts. We would not be able to do that, if we spent all our money on take-outs, meals out, drinking in bars. Being able to leave our children and grandchildren a substantial amount in the future lights us up, being able to help others who need it lights us up. This would not be possible if we got caught up in the "spend everything we make" and "buy it because it's cheap, not because we actually need it" mentality.

Rethinking security

Most people think that their job and their house give them the security and the certainty that they need. But if your company goes under, starts making job cuts, or finds someone younger or cheaper to replace you, or the company closes down branches, how secure will you feel? If after three months, you still haven't got a new job that replaces the income that you are used to and you start to fall behind on your mortgage payments and your bank starts sending you red letters, how secure will you feel then?

If you have an accident, restricting you from working for a while, the basic wage might cover some of your costs, but if you were used to getting the extra overtime to pay your bills, how certain are you going to be about paying the next bill and putting food on the table?

If the utility companies hike up your bills, and you were Just Over Broke in your job, barely keeping afloat, without a minor safety net of say £300 to pay for any repairs or unexpected items, how would you manage to pay out an extra £200 each month to cover these essential bills. How secure are you going to feel?

People call us crazy and see our life as full of uncertainty, with no security, not knowing where we are going to live next. In the beginning, we didn't even know where our next meal was coming from. And we were also homeless once too. But that was down to a lot of bad luck over the week, which we now know could have been avoided with the lessons we have learnt and share within this book (you can read about what happened in chapter 12).

Even before we started travelling, before we created this lifestyle, we had times when we couldn't afford to go grocery shopping and had to go without or make do with what we had. That is what started this journey, because we knew we didn't want this to keep on happening, we knew we had to change something. Our travelling lifestyle did not get us into a hopeless situation. This happened before our lifestyle change, when we were working 8am to

6pm, renting a house, having a car, and paying multiple bills each and every month. And having way more month left at the end of the paycheck.

Is a house asset or liability?

If you think that having a house is an asset, your house isn't an asset until you sell it. And then once it's sold, it's not yours. The definition of an asset is something that makes money, gives you money each month. A house does not do that. It's somewhere where you live. Yes, you need somewhere to live, but having a big house is only an asset once you sell it and it gives you a return, and once you've to sold it, it's not yours anymore. And if it is to pass down, as an inheritance, you've then got to pay taxes and property taxes, et cetera.

So a house is a liability, as you've always got to pay for it. So boilers, heating, pipes, painting, decorating, repairs. And even when you come to sell it, you have to put so much into it before you can actually sell it, if you want a good price, or you can sell it as it is, at a lower price. And then you haven't got the best investment or best asset that you actually want it for. Then you've got market fluctuation. If you sell it at the wrong time in a market, that's not such a good investment after all, is it?

With the life that we have created, we don't have to pay out extortionate amounts to live each month, and we do not need to pay for problems that arise such as replacing roofs or fixing leaks. We put our money into our own investments and pensions, and we use that money to build our money machine, which keeps giving back an income, which then gets compounded and compounded each and every month.

It's not just to leave something behind when we die. It's for when we need it, for example, when we retire or when we actually need some more money. We can always produce it, because our money just keeps compounding.

We also have life insurance. So if needs be, our children are all covered. So they'll have everything they need. This isn't a financial book, but there are various ways where you can make money by just investing and putting some money in. And that can keep compounding over and over again. And it will result in far more than a £200,000 to £500,000 house. By the time we both save together, our bank will be worth well over a million pounds. If you've got a million-pound house, well done, but the size of that house will still be a liability because it's going to cost you month in, month out. If you don't sell it at the right time or in the right market, when you need that million pounds, it could reduce down to £800,000, and your children will get much less.

What a sustainable life means to us

Not having a home, not having monthly bills, not having to pay for a car. To us that sounds like a sustainable life. House sitting for free for three to six months at a time is sustainable for us. We might need to spend a few days in a hotel or an Airbnb in between houses, but the price of that is certainly a lot cheaper than having to pay utilities and bills each and every month.

Average monthly bills in the UK amount to £1,000 to £2,000 per month which adds up to £12,000 to £24,000 per year.

We thought that even if we could only house sit for nine months out of 12 and had to pay for somewhere to stay for three months, we would still be better off. A hotel, say a Premier Inn in the UK or an Airbnb in Europe, would cost about £1,000 a month and that would include all bills, internet, and probably the use of a pool. And even if the flights to get there cost £1,000 (by the way, this would be a lot to pay for flights for the four of us), it would still be a great option, and there are so many even cheaper options available.

- £1,000 x 3 months for accommodation
- £1,000 for flights
- Total £4,000
- Saving of £8,000 to £20,000 per year (if we house sit the rest of the year)

Remember to pay yourself / Safety net

When we realised how much we were saving, we worked really, really hard to create our brand, to create our business and to create an income. What we did, which was a little overzealous, was to use every penny we made that we didn't need for the purpose of creating our business to pay off the debt. We paid it all off. But we didn't leave ourselves with anything spare. We just were so intent and so driven to clear the debt we had, we never saved anything or put anything aside for a rainy day.

That's one of the things if I was to do this again, I would tell myself, "Don't pay it all off at once. Save some for you, put some away." Make sure you have access to an emergency fund. So if ever anything does go awry, and we have some funny stories about Airbnbs and other things not working out, you need that backup just in case.

These upsets caused us to be super resourceful and we'll go deeper into the stories as we go through the book. Don't do what we did and throw everything back into the debt. Be a little bit selfish, look after yourself a bit, indulge in some self-care, especially if you have a family, and put enough money aside to cover the cost of a couple nights' accommodation, anywhere in the world, to be sure that you don't ever get stuck.

We value certainty and security – we are not irresponsible – but we also value variety. Doing the same thing in the same job, staying in the same house for 20, 30, 50 years, no thank you. For us, that would mean boredom, depression, life passing us by. It would make us feel old before our time and like we were not living to our full potential.

"Growth is just outside of your comfort zone."

Even if you only try it for a year... Just Do It

You can check out *Security and certainty* here.

Discover your potential sources of income!

Activities.foreverfamilyforeverfree.com/destiny

CHAPTER 5

Earning An Income Online

There are many ways to earn an income while travelling, but before we take a look at some of these, we highly recommend that the first thing you do if you are thinking of taking on this lifestyle is to read *The 4-Hour Work Week* by Tim Ferriss

This book helped us to really change our thinking and our mindset. There's lots of controversy around this book about whether you can really have a four-hour work week or not. And even if you take out the fact that it may take more than four hours, the author helps you break down the process of going from a full-time employed job somewhere to working remotely, to outsourcing the easy tasks and duties, giving you less and less work to do, whilst travelling the world. His approach allows you to be anywhere, which means that your outgoings could drop drastically, yet you will still be creating an incredible income.

So many people thought our idea was such a farfetched dream and a fantasy. They could never imagine being able to do what they do from the comfort of their own home, let alone anywhere in the world. One thing this pandemic has taught everybody, or at least a lot of people, is that they can work from home. I know some people weren't able to work from home, but so many were. Their companies created ways. They found ways. They all discovered, tried and tested all these new ways, allowing people to work from the comfort of their home.

So as long as you have internet access, you can work anywhere. As much as the pandemic has shut things down, it's also opened people to the realisation that this really is possible.

And remember, don't get caught up trying to replace your current income, because your outgoings will change. If your outgoings are going to be a lot lower, then you can create a new income target.

You don't necessarily need your own business

So many people think they've got to start from scratch, build a business, build a brand, to make enough money just to cover all their bills, and then loads more to be able to save and travel and do all these crazy things. Remember, if you can bring your outgoings way down, you don't need to work as hard. You don't need to make as much money. It suddenly becomes an achievable goal rather than a life-long dream.

Your job is not the only way you can create money. There are so many different ways you can get out there and make the money you need to live this lifestyle.

You can create your own business if you know what you're doing, or if you have the funds to get yourself an incredible coach. Remember, if you're looking for a coach, always get someone who's living the life you want to ensure they're giving you the right advice.

Affiliate marketing

You can do affiliate marketing, which is where, if you really like what someone else is doing, you can help them sell their products or services, say their coaching services, whatever it is, and you get paid a percentage of each sale, which is a really clever way of earning money without needing a business.

Even with Amazon, you could earn between 1% to 10% of the purchase price of any item bought through your affiliate link. It's easy to do. You can just put an affiliate link into a Facebook post, and you'll make money if it's clicked on and the people buy.

Teaching online

If you have a specialised skill that you can teach people online, you can create your own online programme. This is an incredible business that you can go straight into and people will pay you good money for your expertise. So many people hold back because they don't think they're the expert yet. You only have to be one chapter ahead of the person you're teaching to make a difference and help them get to where you are today.

Teaching online plus affiliate marketing

So, if you are an electrician and you are teaching people how to change a plug or fix something in their trip box and you can do this on your Facebook page or YouTube channel, you can potentially make money by providing an Amazon-affiliated link to any of the tools or equipment that they're going to need. People are always searching on YouTube for 'how to' videos – how do I change an RCD plug inside my house or how do I fit something? If you can provide the answers to such questions, then on your free video, in the top right-hand corner, you could set up an affiliate link to buy the RCD plug or a certain tool you recommend.

This could be done for any trade, including plumbing, mechanics, anything. If you're a mechanic or a chef and you are at home because your business has closed down, you can make 'how to' videos. How to change a light bulb on a BMW X5. How to bake a six-layer cake. How to clean out the U-bend in your sink. If you've got any skills like that, you can put them on YouTube. People are always searching for how to do things themselves. If you can help them, and then give advice on a product or tool, and have a link ready, they can go straight to Amazon and buy what they need. You have helped them and made some money in the process, all from a 5 to 10-minute video. The good thing with that is that you do the work once, and then get paid again, and again, even while you are sleeping.

YouTube is almost as big as Google for searching things and people will search for anything on YouTube because they want to be able see how to do it themselves. They want to be able to save money from having to call out a trades person, and if it is a 10-minute fix, they won't need to wait in all day for someone to come around. I have fixed toilet flushes, a fan in my laptop, a toaster, all from watching a 'how to' video on YouTube – although, I don't recommend repairing electronic components yourself, as things can go wrong.

While this isn't a business coaching book, I just want to say that when creating your own business and brand, and things like this, consistency is key. Don't worry about clicks and likes. In the first few days, consistently posting, sharing and interacting is key to building your brand and your business. So regularly post helpful, informative blogs, videos, Facebook messages, etc. so that people can get to know and trust you and your business.

You don't need to be an expert

Don't think you have to be an expert either. There are videos going viral right now that were made by ordinary people doing ordinary things. There's one guy who grew up without a dad. He didn't learn all the things a dad would teach his son. How to shave, how change the oil in his car, how to check the oil even. All these simple things that a dad would normally show him just in everyday life, he didn't have. So he created a channel for other lads who don't have that.

He is a marketing genius, obviously, because he's created this amazing thing, but he's not an expert in any set skill. He's just doing what he was missing, thinking, "Oh, I can help a few people out there who are like me", and it has blown up. You don't have to be the best of the best of the best. You just have to have the idea and the courage to put it out there.

YouTube

With YouTube, you can make money from advertising once you get enough likes and subscribers. That can be hard going at the beginning, but with the affiliate links as well and the YouTube ranking, it all adds up. And if you're getting something like $50 to $100 a week, just from some videos, that is still a lot of money, especially if you're paying out just $400 to $500 a month in living expenses.

Multilevel marketing

Other ways to make income include multi-level marketing or MLM. MLM is where you earn commission from directly selling the products of a company to your friends and family, as well as earning commission on the sales made by the team you build up. Lots of people get caught up with the idea that MLM a pyramid. I'm sure there are some bad apples out there who misuse the concept, but if you find yourself a good company, it can be a really great way to build a team and make an income. It does take a lot of determination, a lot of drive, but if you're a people person, you can really make your team and sales grow quickly.

We actually started off with an MLM business with Forever Living. We still use their products to this day, and our most successful moment was when I'd had enough of doctors. I had a little baby all bunged up with a cold and the doctors were like, "Well, it's just one of those things. Nothing you can do." As a new mum, seeing my baby like this, and having not slept much, I did a rant, because I used to blog back then, and I did this whole mummy rant and someone recommended using Forever Living's Aloe Heat on the soles of his feet, on the arches. I tried it and within two hours, he was completely clear and absolutely fine.

So I did a whole rant saying doctors don't know what they're talking about. Here is something you can do to help your babies. Use this stuff. I wasn't even trying to sell it. Honestly, I was just a really grumpy, overtired mum, and the blog just went crazy and was incredible. So just being real, just being you, just sharing is when magic can happen. You just need to have the courage to get out there and share.

Online marketing

You also have online marketing. If you are someone who loves sales or has worked in online marketing in any way, you can do incredible things. You can charge for your expertise. You can create courses. You can work one-on-one with businesses, brands and people to help them grow their business. Online marketing is probably one of the most sought-after trades and it also can run alongside affiliate marketing.

Affiliates

We use affiliates, and when they sell one of our book programmes that cost $5,000, they earn $2,000 per programme that they sell. So it's worth it for them to go out and put the money in their online marketing campaigns, because even just one sale is worth $2,000. Now with this lifestyle, you can live off that, save money and pay off your debts. So really get out there, really do some research, ask around, and talk to other people doing what you want to do.

Get the right advice for you

If you are a mum with a few kids, don't go to the single 20-year-old guy and ask him how he made his millions. He has time. He has energy. He is full up. He gets to lie in. He gets to do what he wants to do. He has no one relying on him. While he might be incredible at what he does and gets great results for some people, you want someone who understands your lifestyle, your dream and can help you reach your goals in a way that you can achieve them.

Equally, if you're a happy-go-lucky couple, haven't got kids and are just getting started, you might not necessarily need the advice a parent would need, because you have extra time. You have extra energy. You have that extra drive and goals to go and crush it and take even bigger action than maybe a parent would have time for. So find someone doing what you are doing and mirror, match, copy. Model yourself on what they do and how they do it.

FIVVER

Another great resource to use is fivver.com, a website for freelancers, where you can advertise and sell your services. The platform offers everything from graphic design to digital marketing, writing, translation, video and animation, and more. If you've got a skill, you can make money from it. It's called Fiverr because you can sort of sell your beginning product for $5, but then the next level up is whatever price you choose. If you've got skills, you can make lots and lots of money, working from a laptop, working remotely at the time that you choose, as you set your own hours. You can do this from the convenience of your home, or by the side of the pool or swim-up bar, lol. Even if you work for just two out of four weeks, if you add in some income from YouTube, plus your affiliate marketing, you can cover your costs. There are lots of things you can do to add a little bit to your pile.

Online jobs

If you prefer the traditional route, you can always get an online job, whether that's teaching English abroad if you're into teaching, whether that's becoming a travel agent and helping people arrange their travel, or becoming a customer service team member. And there are 'job' jobs out there as well that are online and available to you.

The main thing to remember is that if you were to give up the big house, the cars, all the stuff you own and all the bills you are paying right now, and stay at an Airbnb in a less expensive place, you won't need to earn as much or work as hard as you do now.

How we make it work

We play all day with our kids and we work in the evenings. We've created this life by design. It's not because we're mega, mega rich. It's because we're frugal. We're careful with our money. We have enough time with our children that we're making memories and experiences and creating that amazing, lasting bond.

We also hustle really hard in the evenings. We work our bums off. We add massive value. We serve our clients with all our heart to make that money, to make that difference. This is how we were able to pay our debt off in just three years, whilst travelling with two children. If we can do that, I believe you can do anything.

> *Whether you are creating a new business or taking your current business to the next level, Kath is an awesome lady who helps you fall in love with your business. She has an awesome book and worksheets where she will help you create your master plan! It is broken down in super manageable chunks and feels as though she is there with you every step of the way. We have included Kath's details in our resource section to help you create your business master plan!*

You can check out *Earning an Income* here.

Watch the guided video and PDF to discover your hidden talents!

Activities.foreverfamilyforeverfree.com/destiny

CHAPTER 6

Children And Schooling

If you have children, you will need to think about their schooling.

First of all, you need to know the rules around schooling in your area, as many places have different outlooks. We're from the UK. In most of the places here, you are free to homeschool. You just need to write a letter to your child's school.

So do be sure to check out what the regulations are in your town, country and location, to make sure that homeschooling is a thing that you can do, which after the pandemic, I think, we all know is now an option.

Then you need to think about the type of homeschooling you want to follow.

There are different ways to homeschool. There's homeschooling, online school, world schooling, unschooling.

We actually world school, going around the world, learning about cultures and history from different aspects, rather than just from the one side offered by schools.

If this is something that interests you, make sure you do your research. There are amazing resources available for all these types of schooling. (You can find more info in the Resources section at the back of the book)

So let's focus on the different ways to school.

Homeschooling

Some people like to homeschool. This is where, just like a teacher, the parents do all the planning. They know what lessons they're going to do. They have workbooks or online resources, and they take their children through so many minutes of maths and English and science and history, and do all amazingly, just like a teacher would do. So it's literally school at home for your children.

Online schools

Some people don't have the time for that, but like the idea of it. So they use online schools. These come in a variety of forms. There's online homeschooling, there are online tutors, there are online teachers, and there are online programmes that will take your children through the various curriculums. If this is something that interests you, make sure you research, as there are amazing, amazing resources for all these types of schooling.

World schooling

What we do now is called world schooling. It so incredible. It's been an absolute joy to watch. Our kids are learning different languages, and learning about different cultures and different backgrounds. When they learn something that's happened, they learn it from five, six different perspectives and come to their own conclusions, rather than the single point of view from the one textbook they would have got in a classroom. It's made them really open-minded, amazing, amazing children.

Wild schooling

You also have wild schooling. This is where you kind of take a step back and just let your children do their own thing, which is why our schooling is a bit of a mix of this. You're not the mum who tells them off for jumping through the leaves or jumping in the muddy puddles. You let them go explore, learn, find things out for themselves, and then come back and tell you what they found and discovered.

Unschooling

If you don't want to do the online schooling, some people do unschooling. It's not about sit-down classes, it's not about sit-down lessons. This is how we started. It is a cross between unschooling and wild schooling. We would just go out and play in nature as much as possible. We were so lucky that we chose to bring our children up in Cornwall. So on our doorstop, we had Heligan Gardens and the Eden Project, which we got locals passes to and it was incredible. It changed with the seasons. We had the beaches, the woods. We were surrounded by such nature and beauty, so we would just go out and play and discover and learn every single day.

Support networks

On social media, there are networks and groups of incredible people who are homeschooling who will give you online suggestions for wild schooling and the most incredible outdoor spaces. There is also lots of community support for people who are unschooling and world schooling. There are huge communities.

When you're doing something different from those closest to you, it can feel lonely. It's hard to ask for advice from someone who doesn't understand. So these groups are a great way to really get an answer or an idea. Even when you're just thinking about it, go have a nosy, go see what it is they're doing with their children and what they're sharing.

How we school

We do a mix of world schooling and unschooling. So when people ask us the basis of our curriculum, we explain that when our kids ask a question, we really answer it. By doing this, they remember it. They keep that curiosity. They keep their imagination. They keep that creativity. They're always creating, discovering, learning. They're like little inventors. They're like the toddlers who take everything to pieces because they want to see how it all goes back together and what's inside. They've never lost that. I feel personally that school kind of clamps down on that and kind of crushes that out of them because they're taught what the schools want to teach them rather than what they want to learn. They've even helped us really get our thirst for knowledge back. So we're always out learning, growing and discovering together. Learning life skills like growing food, permaculture, foraging, composting, building, creating, inventing, saving seeds, meditating, yoga, languages, different cultures, backgrounds and beliefs.

At the end of this chapter, we are going to share with you a quiz to help you discover which style of schooling would suit you best. Now one of the biggest concerns, not that the parents have, but that other people have is, what about socialising? This is the number one question we get asked. I can say with pure confidence that play does not have a language barrier. With play, happiness and smiles, there are no language barriers. And when it comes to foreign languages, I promise you that your children will pick these up quicker than you do. They will learn to say what it is they need to say to join in and play games and to make friends.

And in so many places, the kids are trying to learn English too. So there is a lot of back and forth, and they have beautiful patience with each other and they just deepen their friendships. Our children have friends worldwide. They have friends all over this globe and they're all different ages. They're from all different backgrounds. They're from all different countries. They're not stuck with what everyone thinks traditional school offers in terms of socialising. At traditional schools, kids are with the same peer group with the same ability and the same age for however long they're at school. And they think that's socialising.

You want kids who can roll around and play with a toddler on the floor. You want the kids who are amazing with their own peer group. You want the kids who are amazing so they can go and hold adult conversations. They can go speak to their grandparents and hold those conversations. I know we travel. We go to many events and our children can hold all those conversations. They're happy to play around on the floor. They're happy to be with their own friends, but they can hold some amazing and deep conversations with grown-ups to the point that adults look at me like, "I can't believe I'm having a chat and it's with a kid this young." Socialising is what you make it. So if you are a little introverted, like David, it may push you out of your comfort zone a little to be sociable in a different culture with a different language, because you have to lead by example.

I'm very extroverted. I say hello and good day to everyone we meet in every language. And I'm always trying my best to be out there, be friendly and make a difference. So my kids naturally have that confidence within them.

Rules around homeschooling

When it comes to looking into the rules of homeschooling, please do your research. Don't just ask the teachers. I know from personal experience, we've had parents who've been told that they can't homeschool, it's illegal. The teachers have told them it's illegal.

Remember, your child in that school is worth money to that school. They don't want to be the school that you left. They lose funding. It doesn't look good if they've got people leaving their school. So do not research it through the teachers, do your own research. In the UK, and most places, it's as simple as you giving a week's notice in writing to the school. And that is it.

It's not as dramatic as people seem to think and seem to fear, but it seems to be a big thing that teachers don't always get on board with. And don't always support. That's because there are some bad apples out there, like with anything. You hear about cowboy builders, but not all builders are bad. So remember that you need to research it correctly.

Find out from government websites in your area. The rules will be clearly stated there. In some places, you can homeschool, but you have to cover a certain curriculum. It's different in different states across the US and different countries across Europe. But for most places in the UK, you just have to submit your written notice and then you are good to go.

	PROS	CONS
Wildschooling/Unschooling	Kids lead learning	You won't always know all on the topics so can research with them
	Kids interested and retain info learnt	They may learn different areas at different stages, some ahead of the norm some not
	Kids discover, explore and learn on their own or their way	Not up to date on target matching the curriculum
	Kids learn how to think and how to find the answers	'normal peoples' judgments and misunderstandings
	Really fun, lots of outdoor play	
	Learns resourcefulness	
	Learning life skills	
Learning through explore and play	You can guide topics and learning by what you set up and plan for	Having to think of activities everyday
	Get to play alongside your kids	Guiding them your way may not always work
	Can observe how they learn	If using resources costs can add up
	Can be indoors outdoors or anywhere else	May need a routine to make this work well
	Super fun	
Planned curriculum I learn and teach	Keeps them following along with school kids	Having to learn understand and plan lessons
	Mainstream people more accepting	Teaching the curriculum instead of interests can be faced with kids not wanting to do it
	If short term, they can drop straight back into school	Not following the kids interests and excitement
	Keeps the kids in a routine	Trying to teach not understanding how they learn
		Routine is needed
		High expectations on yourself and the kids
Follow homeschool curriculum with tutors	Skilled professionals teaching your kids	Kids taught what to think not how to think
	No lesson planning for you	Expensive
	Mainstream people more accepting	Finding the best tutors right for your kids
	If wanting to go back to school will make the transition easier.	Kids spending all their learning time on a device indoors
		Strict routine

How long is the homeschooling day?

I'm going to quickly touch on the subject of how many hours a day of schooling we do. If you're doing homeschooling or online schooling, this will vary. If you are wild schooling, unschooling, world schooling, there are no sit-down classes, weekly timetables or even school holidays.

People ask us, "Do you stop schooling for the six-week summer holiday or for the two weeks over Christmas?" For us, learning never stops. When it's natural, when it's based on life skills, when you're learning through life, you don't turn the lessons on and off. Every moment is a moment to learn something new, to discover something new, to create something new. So we never turn learning off – it is about life skills, helping prep our food, helping building a fire, gardening, growing the fruit and vegetables that we eat from seed.

Tyler learnt fractions on a walk we used to do. We used to walk four kilometres into the local town to go to the market and he would ask, "How long have we got to go? How far have we gone?"

In the mud with a stick, I'd show him, "This is about a quarter of the way, this is about half the way. We're about three-quarters of the way now." He learnt with a stick in the mud, doing that journey over and over, all these different breakdowns of fractions. Tegan loves her food. She learnt fractions with pizza.

"I don't know how to do fractions."

"Okay. There's one pizza and four of us, and if we all have two pieces each."

She learnt really quickly to know how many slices of pizza she was going to get. It's play. It's fun. They enjoy it. They have such a thirst for knowledge. My little girl went to school for the first couple years. It's a messy background. Those who know our story will know that we couldn't homeschool or world school her until we'd won the adoption. And then we had to wait for a six-month settling-in period.

So that time she legally had to be in school and it wasn't until a year or a year and a half later that she realised she'd been out of school for over a year. She looked at me one day and said, "Mummy, we haven't done any schoolwork yet."

I said, "Oh man, have I forgotten to do that?"

Then we were doing an activity and playing, and it's like I got caught out.

She said, "Mummy, we learn through playing, don't we? You teach us when we're playing. We don't even know we're learning." And it was like she'd discovered this amazing secret.

I jokingly said, "Oh man, I'm going to have to stop. Let's go back to lessons."

And she said, "No, no, no. I like it. Let's keep doing it like that."

When she and her brother became aware that I was teaching them through play, the quality of their questions got better. They would ask more questions. They would go deeper into the subject and topic, realising that they're learning, not just playing.

It's been a really incredible journey. When you think about how many hours to put in, if you are unschooling, wild schooling, world schooling, it's endless. It never turns off. It's nothing like school. It's just life. They're living and learning and growing at every moment. From the first moment when they get up and have breakfast, to just before they go to bed, there are questions and answers, ideas and solutions that are being shared. Instead of learning between 9am and 4pm, and then learning stops, knowledge is always there to be gained.

Our children's point of view

We thought it would be a good idea to get our children's point of view. We want this to be a helpful guide, something that you can take action on if you wish and be able to change your lifestyle. Tegan was seven and Tyler was only four when we left our farmhouse in Cornwall, so the downsizing bit Tyler is a bit vague is on, but he does explain how he feels now though. We have tried to ask them the questions your children are likely to ask or want answers to.

Tegan's thoughts at age 13

What were your thoughts when you could only take toys enough to fill a case?

A bit sad because we had so many amazing toys, but I was also excited because I knew we were going to have fun times, and now I feel it was worth giving up those toys for all the adventures we have had.

When Mummy was giving away your toys to strangers how did that feel?

Happy, because we were helping others that didn't have so much, it made others happy and that was magical to help others.

What was it like saying goodbye to the house that you grew up in?

It was a bit hard because it was my first real home, we had a tree house, a pet bunny, our own rooms that were magical, but it was fun because a new adventure awaited.

What was it like saying goodbye to Pops, Carl, and Gill (the rabbit)

Really sad because they always came over and saw us, we had Gill to play with. Uncle Carl and Pops were so much fun with us, we always knew what they were doing, and they used to know what we were up to, and now we connect on the internet phone calls to catch up instead and we could tell them all about the fun we were having. I miss them but love that Uncle Carl comes and joins us sometimes.

Thoughts on packing up and moving to different places in London?

It was fun and after a while we started getting used to it, and we got to see new places. After a while I found it better than living in one house because there are always amazing new things to see in new homes.

How was your time when we spent in the hotel opposite the airport?

So fun. Multiple times a day we got to see the big planes taking off, and we wished we would be on those planes, we would pretend we were on them going somewhere amazing and we really did it, we made our dreams come true.

How is it meeting new children, do you make friends easily?

Sometimes it's a little hard with different languages, but they always help me, and I help them, we teach each other our languages, they have new games we haven't played before. Sometimes I get a little awkward, but Tyler is fearless at making friends and he helps me.

If you could give two pieces of advice for other children whose parents are thinking the same of travelling full time, what should the kids ask to do, or not do?

Have fun, enjoy it, always try, and learn some basics of each language, hello, please and thank you. When you use these few words, the people always want to help you and they help teach you even more words. In Romania when we first got there I didn't know much and after trying with people, they helped me and after a few weeks, I could order things from the shop and talk to the neighbours.

How about when we got to our first house in Spain by the beach and the swimming pools?

Exciting, finally on a plane, we wished it every day and now we were getting on the plane, it was exciting, and we got to see daddy every day, it was amazing.

When we leave different places and get rid of clothes and toys so it all fits in the case again, how does that feel?

Exciting because the next place we get new things to match the place we are visiting, in Spain we had outdoors and beach toys, in Romania we got a sledge and snow gear, and where it was smooth and flat, we had roller blades.

Getting to a new place with new bedrooms and surroundings, how does that feel?

A little weird, but so exciting, it's new and different.

Do you prefer to stay in a new place for 1 month, 3 months, 6 months or 1 year?

I like about 3 months because 6 months to a year feels like a long time and I am ready to see somewhere new. 1 month doesn't feel long enough to really get to know the place.

What are the good things about moving often?

Always make new friends, learning different things, I have friends all over the world and each friend I learn something new from.

What are the bad things about moving often?

I don't always like the colder countries.

If you could wave a magic wand, what would you ask for (and don't say a unicorn)?

I would ask for a new camera to take photos. Every year, Mummy does this amazing thing, she takes photos from all the places we went to and the people we met and makes us a poster of these pictures, so we always remember all our adventures. This is a great thing that I really love.

Tyler's thoughts at age 9

What were your thoughts when you could only take toys enough to fill a case?

I do not remember

When Mummy was giving away your toys to strangers how did that feel?

I do not remember

What was it like saying goodbye to the house that you grew up in?

Exciting

What was it like saying goodbye to Pops, Carl, and Gill (the rabbit)

I do not remember, but I get sad because I want my bunny every day, but it's great to have pets all over the world.

Thoughts on packing up and moving to different places in London?

Weird because we hadn't done it before.

How was your time when we spent in the hotel opposite the airport?

Good, we sometimes went down for breakfast, I got to see all the planes, I had so much fun in the rooms, I loved that we used the swimming pools.

How is it meeting new children, do you make friends easily?

Fun and easy, you just need to kick a ball over to someone and they will play with you. We meet lots of nice kids.

If you could give two pieces of advice for other children, whose parents are thinking the same of travelling full time, what should the kids ask to do, or not do?

Be helpful, especially on moving day, share your adventures and have a Kindle for all your books. I only bring the toys I love best and play with lots, if I don't play with them, I realise I don't need them anymore.

How about when we got to our first house in Spain by the beach and the swimming pools?

The pools were chilly, but good to have Daddy home every day, that was my biggest wish.

When we leave different places and get rid of clothes and toys so it all fits in the case again, how does that feel?

Fine because that's not we need at the next country, it's just stuff.

Getting to a new place with new bedrooms and surroundings, how does that feel?

Exciting, I want to explore it. I feel happy and safe because I have my family with me.

Do you prefer to stay in a new place for 1 month, 3 months, 6 months or 1 year?

Depends on where we are, I love staying where there are swimming pools, hot tubs, snow, trampolines, great sunshine. It's nice to move and change.

What are the good things about moving often?

It's great to go to new places, some with snow, some with sun. I like exploring.

What are the bad things about moving often?

Don't have our own pet. But we have different pets to try and love.

If you could wave a magic wand, what would you ask for (and don't say a unicorn)?

I would ask for millions, so we can travel on private planes and explore even more, go on even bigger adventures like safaris.

David's perspective

Before when I was working and commuting to work, I was away for 10 hours a day. And most times, the children were in bed before I left in the morning and by the time I got back. So I didn't get to see any of their schooling or what needed to be done. Since we've been travelling, I get to be there first hand, helping them with any equations or questions or any research that we're doing. This has brought us much

closer together. Being there first hand, answering questions, if I don't know the answer, I know where I can find it. And that's also a valuable resource to have. Even grown-ups don't know all the answers. If we teach our children that if they don't know the answer, they need to know where to find it and need to look at a variety of resources rather than coming up with the first answer given and believing that is true, then we are teaching them to think for themselves, which is truly a great asset.

What was really incredible was that before David stopped working and joined us, he only ever saw the results. So he would see our kids changing and learning, and their conversations and their vocabulary just used to blow his mind. Every day, he could point out something new that just wowed him about our children. I thought I was helping to build an incredible bond between Daddy and his children, because I would let them stay up later than they probably should have because I wanted them to have that hour every day with Daddy. So David would come home, bless him, probably exhausted, play full out for an hour with our kids. Then I'd go put them to bed, sit with them, calm them down, get them to sleep while Daddy had an hour or so to then chill out from work. I thought this created an incredible bond, which I'm sure it did, compared to some dads who work all the hours and don't purposely make this time with their children.

But after three weeks, a month maybe, of him being with us full time, to see the way our children then bonded with Daddy, it almost had me in tears. I felt like I'd almost kind of failed them before because they never had a bond like this. It also made me cry with absolute gratitude that in such a short time, we were able for him to fire his boss and jump into this lifestyle full-time. He got to experience our kids grow up. The reason why we made a rush to do this is because we didn't want to wait until we had money in the bank, because children can't wait. They won't wait until you've got the money. They're growing up now. I wanted David to experience everything I was experiencing. I wanted the children to know who their Daddy was. I wanted us to watch them grow, learn and develop together.

Every time they have a little breakthrough, and their eyes grow to the size of jam jar lids, it's really magical. And if you've had those moments with your children, you'll know this for yourself. From simple things like speaking their first words and taking their first steps, to them discovering something new, doing some little crazy science experiment and finding the outcome, figuring something out for themselves and seeing it work, or not working, and them changing their approach and trying again and again, and learning that things don't always happen first time, to know that things might need improvement, is so rewarding.

One example is the Apple phone. Apple is on version 13. Had the company waited to get it right first time, they may never have launched. It is only by using the phone, experiencing the problems, and seeing what needs to be adjusted that you can keep on improving.

To see how we are bonded with our children, to see how Daddy has bonded with his children now, that has been priceless. We started when our youngest was four and our eldest was only seven, and we felt it wasn't soon enough. It has been magical. I am so grateful we did not wait until we could afford it, until we had enough money, because David would have missed out on so much.

You can check out *Children & Schooling* here.

Take the quiz to discover which style of schooling would suit you and your children best. Also talk to your children, get them involved in your plans and try to answer any questions that they might have.

Activities.foreverfamilyforeverfree.com/destiny

We love to give back, and support those who are out there trying to make a positive difference to this world.

In this book we are supporting an incredible young man who is on a mission to prevent suicide in university students, those away from home needing extra support. I know he will create huge changes and incredible results. If you have children that may one day be off to Uni, or you can help and support this mission in any way, please reach out and connect with the amazing Andrew Porteous.

CHAPTER 7

Minimalism & How To Start?

Minimalism. If you want the freedom to live a nomadic life, then you'll need to learn to travel light. So many people think there's a right way to do it – to the point that they'll even join groups and ask other people for their opinion. It is different for everybody.

To us, minimalism is living with what you need, rather than what you might want. We've learnt to live for the experience and a sense of freedom, and not the material items we own. We've learnt not to be attached to things, knowing there's always better around the corner.

Becoming minimalist wasn't an easy process. We had a beautiful, four-bedroom farmhouse with two kids' rooms and a playroom, a large shed and outdoor spaces. And we had so much stuff – a piano, an electric massage bed, you name it. I should say, I had so much stuff. David not so much. I had clothes from when I was a teenager. I hoarded so much stuff. I kept everything that my kids had ever touched, because it just was magical. I love keeping memories.

I found it really challenging to let go of so much stuff at the time – especially some of my favourite things, even though I knew I'd never get back into them so I'd never wear them again. It brought me to tears to think of giving this stuff away. It may sound a little crazy, but I found the easiest way to part with these items was to give them a hug, thank them for the joy and pleasure they'd brought me, and then let them go. But my goodness, it was so tough.

From a four-bedroom house to four suitcases

When we first thought about travelling, I was thinking that we needed to get it down to four cases. And I thought four full-sized cases at the time.

We took it room by room, shelf by shelf, drawer by drawer, cupboard by cupboard, wardrobe by wardrobe, step by step. It took us four months to go from a four-bedroom farmhouse full of stuff to four big suitcases.

The beautiful thing is we started to look at things differently. We gave so, so much away. Most of our stuff went to charities and families in need. We took bags and bags of stuff to the local air ambulance charity stores, thrift stores, to try and give back, and make a difference with the stuff we were letting go of.

We were into property then and we knew a family who had relatives coming for Christmas and they didn't even have a dining room table. So knowing that they were going to be out picking up their family, we got them this massive table and chair set, set it up in their home, laid out all their plates and cutlery, with crackers and everything, and left a little card that said, "Merry Christmas, hope you have a great time."

Keep the things that mean something

Anyone with kids knows that everything means everything to them. They did this once with this toy. They did this once in this outfit. I'm not telling you to throw away all your stuff and all your memories. Not at all. We still have a storage locker, which is a bit like the Ritchie Rich vault. If someone broke into it and hoped to acquire wealth, they'd be so hugely disappointed, because it just contains trinkets and things that hold little memories for us. Not only from our travels, but from our children's childhoods.

Learning what travelling light really means

The amount we gave away and cleared was incredible. It's hard to describe, but once it was done, it felt so freeing. It emptied and cleared our minds. It took a weight off our shoulders. So all this stuff we were holding onto was just lifted and gone. It was such an amazing gift and a side effect that we didn't know or expect when it came to letting go of all these things.

When we first travelled, we still had so much stuff. I kind of laugh at us now, because we thought we'd cut everything down to the bare basics. We still had these massive cases and all these backpacks, and whatever we could carry in carrier bags. It was ridiculous. But we were so proud of ourselves. We did a 'what's in the case' video when we landed in our first country, which was Spain, and it was my little boy's case. Now when I rewatch it, I find it so funny that we thought we had so little. It seems like so much stuff compared to what we take now.

It was not until we moved a few times that we started to realise that there were things that we'd never even taken out of our cases and that we were never going to use. The more experience you have, the more you start to realise that you need so much less than you think you need. When you have little ones, they do need a few more tops and outfits than us adults need, because they do make more mess more often. Now, me and David only have four or five tops at the most.

We've had people say to us, "Oh my gosh, don't you run out of things to wear?" Well, there's this cool invention that's available in most places around the world called a washing machine. You just wash your clothes when you need to.

Think about when you go on a two-week vacation, you pack for every scenario, and you take a big case. You also take hand luggage and your bag or your backpack. Then you go to this amazing place. You live in one swimsuit during the day and wear a beautiful dress in the evening, or maybe you have a couple dresses. If you're a guy, you maybe only wear a couple shirts and a pair of shorts. Nothing else comes out of the case. Yet, you've carried it all that way. And for what?

When it comes to toiletries, we actually have one natural product that we all use in the shower for body and hair. Just one, for all four of us, because it's an adaptogen, so it adapts to our hair type, our skin type, and it's magical.

We all use one fluoride-free toothpaste. In a typical family home, there may be two or three types of shampoo, two or three types of conditioner, two or three types of soap, and two or three types of toothpaste for different ages. Then you've got hair products and deodorants, and it's overwhelming. We look at life so differently now to the point that when we go into a supermarket and see two aisles just for shampoo and conditioners, we ask, "Why? Why is there a need for such a huge choice of soap? It's just soap."

So the more practice you have at this, the better you get. But I don't want to overlook the fact that the first clear-out is not easy, especially if you've hoarded for a long time. Over time, it definitely changes. And you start to realise how little you actually need to live.

Pack for the present

As parents, we normally buy things for our kids, thinking, "Oh, they'll grow into that. I'll buy the bigger size so we can keep it for next season."

Like most kids, our kids are wearing out and growing out of things all the time, but we only take with us what fits them now.

If we need to buy new things for them, we go to websites like eBay, which are magical places for buying huge bundles of clothes for very little. So when we're visiting the UK or we're getting somewhere close, we will order a huge bundle of clothes to fit the kids right there and then.

It might cost us a pound or a dollar an item, or less. A lot of it is from UK brands such as Next, M&S, Monsoon. These beautiful, amazing brands come at £1 an item, because people bought these clothes for their children for special occasions, then never let them wear them again because they were so worried about them getting damaged or stained, and then they've outgrown them. So we get these beautiful bundles of clothes for crazy prices. If our kids go out and stain and wreck them, not that we want them to, but if they do, there's no drama.

We get full wear out of our items because we only have a few. So they get used, they get worn well, they get really lived in, and then they get given away or recycled.

Who needs old technology?

So many of things that we have now and that seem so important may not be so important in the future. When we started this journey, we kept CDs, DVDs, all these things. They don't really exist in today's world. Who do you know with a DVD or CD player now? They are almost completely irrelevant. So in the beginning, this may seem really crazy tough, and you might want to store loads of stuff in friends' and family members' attics, or take out massive storage units, but I promise you, the more you travel, the more you will revisit your storage unit, and the smaller your stash will get. We're constantly adding things from our travels and adventures to our unit, and it's still declining in size as we ask ourselves, "Why are we keeping this? How is this ever going to serve us?"

About storage units

I want to touch on storage here. So we do use a storage unit. If you are thinking of doing the same, I would get quotes and not necessarily choose the cheapest, but a quality company with a great reputation. When it comes to storage insurance, don't take it out with the company that provides your storage. Get your own personal insurance. It will cost a lot less than what you'll pay through the storage company.

The funny thing is, at the beginning, we had two 10-square-foot storage units, because we thought we needed all this stuff. We were chasing the sun around the world for about two years. Then we came back to the UK. We caught up with lots of friends and family, and went back to our storage unit to put some of our travel memorabilia in it.

David and I just kept looking at each other asking, "Why did we keep this?" We couldn't fathom certain things we were keeping. We decided, "Okay, we need to have a clear out. We're paying for two units. We don't need most of this stuff." We actually got it down to just one square-foot storage box, which is approximately three feet by three feet by three feet.

Now, we just have the one and each time we visit, we're adding to it from our travels, but removing items at the same time. Why are we keeping all these DVDs? We can stream everything we want from all these amazing streaming services.

10-square-foot storage unit. We had two at the start and after two years, we sorted through and cut it down to one unit.

Books

Before we set out on our travels, we gave our kids a Trunkie each and said, "Go fill it up with your favourite toys. Whatever you can fit in there is what you're going to keep for at least the first couple of moves." It seems like loads now. They both went and filled their Trunkies with books. It broke my heart, because I love books too. I brought them up to love books. But books are heavy. And they take up a lot of space. So we ended up going out and getting them Kindles and downloading their favourite books, so that we could have them with us. Every birthday and Christmas, people ask us, "What do you want?" And we say, "Kindle books, Kindle books, Kindle books." Whenever we go anywhere, if we see books, either in the local language or in English, and we're staying somewhere for a little while, we will happily buy books and then gift them on, because there's nothing quite like holding a physical book.

We do love them. But the kids do have their Kindles because their favourite toys have always been books.

Toys

They have a few toys each that they always take with them, as they are small and can be used in several different ways, to enhance their imagination and creativity. Tyler has small toy cars, mini dinosaurs and animals, walkie talkies, a fidget spinner, some Lego and story dice. Tegan has two puzzles (1,000 pieces and we change these frequently), playing cards, uno card game, Rubix cubes, mini horses, pens and pencils. They have great imaginations and can turn a walkie talkie and a few mini animals into an animal rescue adventure or guided safari tour.

We also make toys and games which double up as arts and crafts. Laura has made them toy kitchens so many times that now the kids can do it themselves, but they go above and beyond, and create restaurant menus and card readers for their customers to pay with.

We all love playing with the story dice, it contains nine dice with six different pictures on each one and you roll them and create a story out of the images you see. The imagination can run wild, and Tyler did give himself nightmares one time when camping with Daddy.

The case for carry-ons

Now, we realise that not everyone's dream life includes a carry-on case. You might want to put your case in the hold. The only reason we chose a carry-on is because I want us to travel light. I want us to be private jet ready. If we're going to be going off somewhere, I want us to be ready to just up and go at a moment's notice. Also, with putting your luggage in the hold when you go on holiday, if they lose your case, you lose all your holiday stuff for the two weeks of your holiday. When you live out of a suitcase, it suddenly becomes much more important for you to keep hold of that case.

We travelled once with a case that went in the hold and it got lost. We got it back a couple weeks later, but they'd actually lost it. Now, a normal person would think, "It's my holiday stuff, it will come back." That's okay if you are on holiday. Our whole lives are in these cases. So we like to carry them on the plane with us. That's the reason why we downsized so much to fit it all into a carry-on-case.

If you need to start with bigger cases, do that, find your flow, find your happy. Something else we do is we live seasonally. We chased the sun for two years. In our carry-on cases, we only had summer clothes. We didn't need to take bulkier winter and autumn outfits, or spring waterproofs. We only had summer clothes, which take up very little room.

Thrift stores

We did then go from summertime to winter in Utah, which was amazing, but really snowy. We went to a thrift store and kitted ourselves out with full-on ski jackets, winter jumpers, everything we needed for the four of us. I think it cost about $70. What was beautiful was we only used them for about a month. Then we went and gave them back to the thrift store in almost the same condition. Now, if we'd hired winter clothing, we'd have been looking at hundreds of dollars a day. If we'd bought it all new, we'd have been looking at spending even more. This way, we felt it was a win-win. We got what we needed for the time we needed it for a sensible price, because remember, we were travelling our way out of debt. We were then able to give it back and help a charity. We were not rich. We had to think about the money we spent, and we loved that we were able to still give back, even though we were on the move. The thrift stores in America blew us away.

When we went to Costa Rica for those few months, a kind of orange, sandy dust got into all our clothes. The washing machine only had a cold wash, which we filled up with a hose pipe. We then had to hand spin our clothes to wring them out. It was tough. And what was so incredible was that it was so hot that the washing was dry before we even got it all pegged out. Amazing. But the orange dust never quite came out. So when we left Costa Rica, we left with almost no clothes. We pretty much had to get rid of all of it because it was all stained orange. The kids were getting to the point of outgrowing their clothes anyway. So we just completely scrapped it all and started again.

We were then flying into LA. We went into a thrift store and got beautiful designer tops and trousers, and skirts and shirts. I'm talking $1, $1.50, $2 per item. I think $2.50 was the most expensive thing that we bought. And we were kitted out in designer gear. No one knows where you've bought your clothes from. If you don't mind not being in this season's fashions, you can get so much more for your money.

When it comes to downsizing, people overcomplicate it. They get in their heads and they stress a little. My challenge to you is to get a carry-on suitcase.

Then put everything you think you'll wear for the next seven days and everything you think you'll use for the next seven days, including personal stuff, in the carry-on case.

Most people think they're going to need to take everything. We take too much stuff when, in actual fact, we tend to wear the same few outfits, the same pair of comfy shoes, the same dress or suit, over and over again. I used to be just as bad. I'd go on a holiday with the biggest case ever and I'd live in two outfits and a bikini. Why do we take all the other stuff? Because we all think, "What in case? What about? What if?"

So I challenge you to put everything you think you'll use this week into a carry-on case and see how much you really have. And do the same for your children and your partner.

Also, you need to think about what else you will need. We carry our laptops with us, so we always have three laptops. The kids have Kindles. We have a massage gun, a poster tube with our yearly photos collage, and David has his A4 canvas and acrylic paints and a cordless glue gun as he loves his art.

Trunkies

As I mentioned, we did start off with Trunkies for the kids. Trunkies are great for holidays, and they're fun and entertaining, but they don't actually hold much at all and our kids outgrew them way too quickly. So they are great for holidays, but not great for our lifestyle.

Recently, I travelled to the UK and as we were downsizing our books again, and they were too good to throw away and a lot of them were great learning-to-read books, I wanted to give them to my sister. So I took them in my carry-on case. Oh my goodness. Trying to put that case in the overhead locker, I had to lift it up onto the chair, then onto the arm of the chair, then onto the back of the chair. I think I'm quite strong, but the case was so heavy to lift up there. I got watched but nothing was questioned and nothing was said. And not only that, I also had a big stash of books in my backpack. So my bag weighed a stupid amount if you include my carry-on and my bag. As long as you're not making it obvious and making a big deal of it, it will be fine. If we can go to that extreme, don't worry about being the odd little bit over.

It's only when your case goes in the hold that they do the checks and the weigh-in, and then check the size of your case before they put the little tag on it. If you are just going straight through customs and passport security, then they only look at your tickets. Then you get straight on the plane. It really is no problem whatsoever. Most airlines don't have a specific weight limit. All they ask is whether you can lift your carry-on into the overhead locker unaided. So as long as you can lift it up, it's not an issue.

The only time heavy luggage does become a problem is if your kids aren't strong enough yet to carry their own cases. I travelled once without David, so there were three of us with three cases. It just happened to be a flight where they took us out onto the tarmac and we had to climb up the steps, rather than board through the tunnel. So there I was on my own with three cases and two kids, and my kids were really small. I could manage two cases, but I still had the third case and the kids to try and get up those dangerous steps into the airplane. So I had to do two runs. Sometimes there's a kind person who will see you struggling and offer to help. I love those people. I am one of those people. If I travel alone, I help any parent who looks like they're struggling with anything, because I've been there. There aren't loads of helpful people around. So if you see people struggling, please help them, and if you are one of those people being helped, please thank those Good Samaritans. They are amazing.

Our kids don't miss out

Even though our kids only have a carry-on case, they do not go without. Wherever we are, we buy toys and experiences to suit where we are. If we're somewhere snowy, we buy winter gear and sledges, and have such an incredible time. When we're somewhere with a pool and on the beach, we buy buckets and spades and floats and fun things for the pool. We often donate these toys before we then travel to the next location.

Romania is the best example of this, because we were staying in a place that was really quite poor. One day, we left a football in the park, and we sat and watched a group of kids come and play. What we found amazing is that when they finished playing, they left the ball there for the next lot of kids. So we bought a few different footballs and put them in different parks all around the area.

Our kids have learnt to not be attached to things and stuff. They never go without, and they do leave things behind, but they're not emotionally attached to them. They're not triggered by any of it. They know stuff is just stuff and can be replaced, whereas the experiences, adventures and time we spend together are magic, priceless and can't be replaced.

You can check out the *Minimalism activities* here.

Watch our video 'what's in the case' from our first trip, thinking that we were travelling light, and a video of how little we travel with now.

Then take the Challenge!

Activities.foreverfamilyforeverfree.com/destiny

Part 2:

Living Your Dream Lifestyle

CHAPTER 8

Travelling Abroad On A Budget

Travel off-peak and book early

We're not the kind of family who is going to haul up in a camper van. That's my bad. I'm a full-time traveller who gets travel sick. So we like to take flights. What is great is that we are not stuck to the school timetable. This allows us complete freedom to choose to fly on whatever dates we want. So instead of having to book a certain date, we can be flexible. So we can go when it's cheap. This year, we've done trips from Europe to the UK for as little as £13 for a round trip. A return flight for just £13 (admittedly, the reason this was so cheap is because I was flying solo and only took a backpack). We've sat on the same plane as all the people who paid £100, £200 more for the same flight. So by being flexible and booking well in advance, you can get the best prices.

Bring food with you

Kids want to eat on the plane. It's the cool thing to do. We recommend buying food for the plane before you fly, but definitely not in the airport. Buy it from a shop and take it with you. You can't take liquids through, but you can take sandwiches, crisps, fruit.

Some countries won't allow you to bring exotic fruits into another country, so double check that before you fly. But you can take a packed lunch for your kids so they can eat on the airplane. Don't pay extortion fees for half a slice of pizza and four chips on the plane.

Car hire

Another great way of saving money is when it comes to car hire. People often pay for excess insurance, which can be a lot per day. And if you're hiring a car for a week or so, it can really add up and double the cost of the car hire. We use an amazing company that provides year-round car excess insurance so that we don't have to pay for it every time we hire a car. We pay for it annually and it covers both of us for the year. It costs less than a $100. If we are hiring a car, we make that back in just one trip, so it is totally worth it if you're going to be hiring cars. (You can find details of this company in the Resources section at the back of the book.)

Buying a car

If you're going to buy a car, say if you're going to be somewhere for six months or longer, it's definitely worth having a local help you buy a cheap run-around. I'm not suggesting that you buy an amazing, up-to-date car. Buying a little run-around can be much cheaper than hiring a car. Just be careful in certain countries about where you buy and how you buy. We're quite lucky in that we were both car mechanics in a previous life, so we know what we're buying.

We actually went back to the UK for three months and rather than hire a car, which would have been quite costly, we put an advert on a local Facebook group where we are from, saying, "Okay, I have a really small budget. I need a car that would just last me three months. What have you got?" We got inundated with responses. We picked up a nice little Skoda for £160. We then taxed it, insured it, drove it for three months, and we actually sold it again online and the new owners picked it up from the airport. So on the day we were to fly out, we agreed to meet them two and a half hours before our flight at the front of the airport at the drop-off place. We literally drove the car to the airport, took all our bags and car seats out of it, gave them the keys, signed over the paperwork, and then they drove it off 20 minutes later. So they didn't have to pay for parking. We didn't have to try and get from the car to the airport once it was sold. It was the most perfect transaction we've ever done. A car for £160 lasted us three months. The buyers actually paid £160 for the car, so we lost no money on it. All we had to pay was tax, insurance and fuel, which we did as monthly costs. So when we cancelled the tax and insurance, we'd only paid for the three months that we had the car. It was one of the best car investments we've ever made.

In our latest deal, we bought a 20-year-old Volvo V70, with 10 months' MOT. We searched eBay, Gumtree and Facebook marketplace for many different cars. We wanted it to be big enough to put all the cases in the boot and to give the children enough space in the back, so there was nothing in the foot wells or on the seats. We wanted a comfortable car as we were travelling around the UK to different house sits and so could be travelling 300 miles at a time, and we wanted it to be under £1,000.

We picked up the V70 for £655 from eBay. If we were to quickly sell it on we-buy-any-car.com in the condition that it would be in when we'd finished driving an extra 4,000 miles and with five months' MOT left, we would get £550. That's five months' worth of motoring for £155 plus tax, insurance and fuel.

Travel Hacks.

Airline luggage restrictions

When looking at carry-on size suitcases, there are different size restrictions for different airlines. Some will be 21.7 inches, others will be 22 inches. This isn't a problem. What we use are fabric cases, rather than the hard plastic ones, so that we can sort of rearrange our content and make it a little bit thicker or a little bit thinner, or make it a little bit longer to fit whatever the airline requires. And you can always take your coat out of your case if need be to make it smaller.

We always travel priority, which means we can take a carry-on case and a backpack each on board. Sometimes we need to use our backpacks if the carry-on allowance is smaller. Another really good trick is that you're also allowed to take on a bag of duty free. We're a bit cheeky and we carry a WH Smith bag with us, because WH Smith is in most airports, especially around Europe. So if things are not going to quite fit in our cases, or our cases are slightly too big, rather than tie our jumpers around our waist and wear our coats where it's hot, we just pop the extra clothing in the WH Smith bag and pretend that we're carrying on duty free, which we're allowed. Having a suitcase with the wheels built into the inside will give you the most amount of room, because you are not losing that extra couple inches along the bottom of the suitcase.

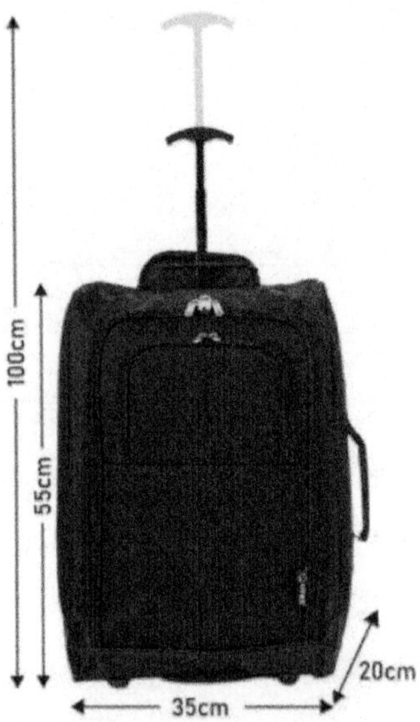

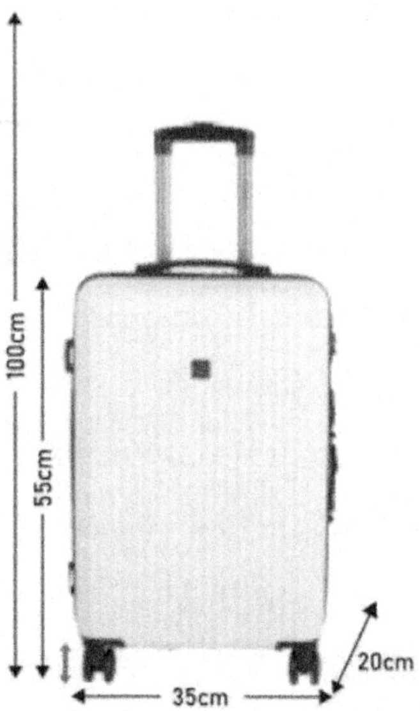

The white suitcase has the wheels connected onto the bottom, so you loose a lot of inner packing space with this style. Also with a hard-shelled case, there is no leeway to bulge out the size a little if you want to make room to put in a jacket. As these are carry-ons and you are in control of your case, there is no need to have a strong pastic casing as it won't be mishandled by the baggage handlers.

What we also found amazing was to use a suitcase that has wheels but also converts to a backpack, so that you can be hands-free if you want. This meant, especially when our children were small, that David could carry a case on his back and handle two cases, while I could manage the fourth case and a kid in one hand, or we could both carry a suitcase on our backs, and manage one case with one arm and a kid in the other arm. I know it sounds exhausting, but it's a way you can make it doable when you've got little kids.

We found these to be the best and the ones that we used were not too pricey. So they're affordable and they are just genius.

You will find links to all of the recommended travel gadgets that we use in the Travel Hacks activity section

When you get to the airport, we recommend never putting your case in the little cage to see if it fits. Don't let them see it that doesn't fit. In the past, we used a suitcase to carry our shopping all the way from the supermarket back home, about a 20-minute walk. But towards the end of the stay, one of the wheels fell off the suitcase. We then had to go and get a new suitcase. We bought a suitcase, not thinking about the size. It was a small carry-on suitcase. Perfect. When we got to the airport, we discovered that it didn't fit in the cage. The wheels were about two inches too long. The case was two inches too high for this particular airline. In the airport, I used my multi-tool screwdriver to undo the screws and take the wheels off, trying to make this suitcase fit in. It never did because there was a big bit of plastic cage around it, which I couldn't get off because it was riveted on. If I'd had a hacksaw, I might have sawn this off, but in the end, we were able to go through the airport and get on the plane. It wasn't an issue. It fit in the top of the overhead lockers just fine and we weren't stopped or questioned. And it was two inches too big. It has been never a problem for us. Dave totally overthinks things, whereas I'm always like, "Eh, it will be fine." It's been proven that, eh, it is fine, especially if you don't have any luggage going in the hold. If you don't have luggage going in the hold, no one checks your carry-on. They don't check to see how much it weighs, unless it looks extreme. I mean, don't go to extremes and try to take a massive case on board. If it's just an inch or a two out, it'll be fine. We can't believe what some people get away with taking on board. So don't push it and get a giant case, but don't worry if your carry-on is a little bit big. If you need to, you can always decant some contents into a duty free bag or put your coat on just to get on the plane. Once you're on board, you're done and everything is fine.

We've never had any issues with them weighing our carry-on luggage. Different airlines have different requirements. But it's never been a problem. So I wouldn't overthink that either. We carry laptops and books and a Revolt massage gun, which probably bring us a bit over the limit.

Our Top Travel Hacks

- Travel off peak
- Book early
- Use a VPN when booking flights from a different country
- Pay for priority when booking flights
- Use carry-ons only
- Just pack what you need now
- Bring food with you on the plane
- Take out annual car waiver insurance to cover the 'excess'
- Enjoy 'free' accommodation by house sitting or house swapping
- Turo car rental – like Airbnb for cars (worldwide)
- Low cost of living in other countries, i.e., Romania and Costa Rica

Plus the list of what we learnt:

- Pay ourselves first
- Create a rainy day fund
- Have spare bank cards
- Know about Weston Union

A bonus hack we just learnt:
"You are allowed to take pillows on the plane, so people stuff their pillows with clothes to save on luggage allowance."

Doug Stone

You can check out *Traveling abroad on a budget* here.

Discover ways to travel that you didn't know existed!

Activities.foreverfamilyforeverfree.com/destiny

CHAPTER 9

Where To Stay.

There are many options – Airbnb, house swapping, house sitting, couch surfing, caravanning, camping. We love house sitting, but we do beautiful hotels and cheeky Airbnb's or we go visit family in between our house sits.

Airbnb

When we first started this adventure, we started with Airbnb because you pay an all-inclusive price, apart from food. And what we found – this is kind of our secret when it comes to Airbnb – is to book by the month, not by the week.

If you book a few days or a couple weeks, you're going to think the prices are kind of crazy. When you book by the month, you get incredible discounts because the hosts are not having to pay the cleaners every few days. They're not having to change the bedsheets every few days. They're saving so much money by not having guests coming in and out, in and out, cleaning, doing the check-ins and check-outs, managing the bookings. So the price drops drastically, and the discount can knock off anywhere from 40% to 80%.

Even if we're going somewhere for just two weeks, we often book for the month because it will work out cheaper to book a month than it will to book two weeks. And what's great about this is that you then have the option to stay longer if you need to or if you want to because you've fallen in love with the place.

What's also really great about Airbnb is that you can reach out to the host before you book. I mean, if it's already 80% discounted, go ahead and grab it.

If it's not discounted or it's not very well discounted, reach out to the owner and private message them. "Hi, I've got ... [whatever your family situation is] ... We'd love to come and stay. We're looking at these kind of dates. What's the best price you can offer me, please?" And see what they can do. Lots of people will offer a much better price than you'll see on the Airbnb website. And then they'll send you a better offer, which still goes through Airbnb, so you're still both protected, but you get a much bigger discount.

When you're booking with Airbnb, you can see a map of the location. You can see what's local to it, you can see what's around. You can see if it's a tourist place or if it's out of the way. Another thing I would really advise – we've accidentally got lucky a couple times without doing this – is to read the reviews. This is so important. If you book an Airbnb and don't read the reviews until later and you see it's completely shocking or they've cancelled at the last minute or there are things really wrong with it, it's really hard to then undo your booking. So be sure to read the reviews before you book.

House swapping

Something we came across that can really get you into the heart of a country, or a city or town, and get to know the people and culture are house sitting and house swapping.

With house swapping, you get to go to another country to stay in someone else's home and they stay in yours. You do a complete swap. If you've ever watched *The Holiday* with Cameron Diaz and Kate Winslett, you'll see that they did a house swap. So you can do this worldwide, and this way you don't have to go all in and give up everything, only to find out a week later that you don't like it, because it's too far out of your comfort zone. You still have your own home to go back to, so it is a great way to test out a new lifestyle.

House swapping is something we looked at when we had our home in Cornwall. And while it was great, we realized we couldn't keep up with the cost of living. If you've got a good, steady income and you just want to travel a lot more, house swapping is an incredible way to get started, to push you out your comfort zone little bit by little bit. We didn't do this, because we were at make or break point, and we decided to burn our boats and go all in.

House sitting

House sitting is where people are going away, and they have a pet that they don't want to put in kennels, or they have a second home that they don't like to leave empty, so they invite people to stay in their house and look after it, and possibly their pets, while they are away.

House sitting is mostly free, although, some people get paid to house sit, which is amazing. We love it when we get a house sit where we don't get paid, but we don't have to pay out. So most of the house sits we have had have covered all the bills, even the Wi-Fi and the internet. Some places have even supplied the firewood if we needed it through the winter. So we've had some incredible house sits that have cost us a minimal amount. It has been one of our favourite resources whilst travelling and trying to pay off all our debts.

We have fallen in love with house sitting, because it takes you into the heart of any culture. Normally, house sits are not on a tourist route, so you get to go into the heart of a village, the heart of a town, in a country you've never been to, and mingle with locals and really enjoy the local culture. Not only are the people who you're sitting for so welcoming, they introduce you to the locals, what's in the area, what's great, what's not so great. You kind of get the rundown on where you are going from someone who lives there, before your adventure begins.

Not only that, you're not in a hotel full of strangers. You're in someone's home and the neighbours get to know you. They know that you've come from somewhere else so if the language is different, they'll be a bit more patient, and if you try, they'll try too. It has been a really incredible experience for us.

And what's also great about it is that, because you're in the heart of the place and not in a tourist location, you save so much money on food.

You have access to local markets, local sellers, all the local produce and shops. You get to really experience the lifestyle, the culture, the way the locals live and the local prices, which are much better than tourist prices, so again, you're saving heaps and heaps of money.

Applying

You won't get every house that you apply for. But the more you get, the easier they are to get, because you build up a track record. So you need to apply for lots of houses and be patient. You need to read what the advert is asking for and make sure you fulfil that in your request. We have specifically changed our profile at times to match the house sit that we want. It was all still truthful, but we really focused on what their needs were and how we could best meet and serve these. Our most recent house sit, we felt, was perfect for us. Our heading was literally, "We are your perfect candidates, look no further." And we actually got that house sit and they said they had many, many enquiries and were just kind of getting flooded. Then they saw our headline come up and thought, "Okay, let's have a look." It intrigued them, and we got the house sit, a family of four winning over a couple.

Homeowners are much more willing to take on a single person or a couple than they are a whole family, so if you don't have children, you will find many more house sitting opportunities than we did. In the beginning, we did get turned down from a few housesits because there was either no room for the four of us, they were looking for a mature couple, or a single person, and some were downright disgusted at the thought of children in their house. Over time, we have received lots of great feedback and testimonials that specifically talk about our awesome children. It is much easier for us to get the sits we request now that we've built up a reputation for being great house sitters. It has now got to the tipping point where we needn't apply, they reach out and request us first.

Camper vans

Another way that people travel with their children is by camper vans or caravans or motor homes, whatever you want to call them. While this is great, and you get to take your home with you and you feel safe because you've got that base, the only problem with it is if something goes wrong with the camper van. You've got to have that backup, that money supply for repairs, maintenance, and to cover the cost of where you're going to stay while your van is being repaired and maintained.

We had friends who travelled all around Europe in a motor home, and while they loved it and it was an amazing adventure, when we compared costs, even when we added in our flights and car hire, they spent way, way more than we spent. I'm talking triple what we spent, because of camp sites costs, road tolls, fuel, maintenance, repairs. Then you've got road tax and car insurance. These were all things that really added up and that we didn't necessarily even expect, because it's not something we were contemplating. Obviously, with house sitting, our outgoings are very, very different.

Camping

When choosing a new lifestyle, it depends how far out of your comfort zone you are prepared to go. If you are a young couple, you can grab a tent and a backpack.

You can go pitch up a tent, even on Airbnb, or just turn up at camp sites. You can get a really great rate if it's just two of you in a two-man tent. And then you'll have access to the site's showers and the toilet facilities.

Couch surfing

There are people who offer couch surfing, where you can go crash on someone's sofa for a few days. Again, they will introduce you to the local area, the local people and what's going on. They know what's going on because it's their area.

Test the waters

So when it comes to making that decision, it's all about how comfortable you are with getting uncomfortable.

And again, if you are really unsure, even though you really want to, but there's something really holding you back, try a house swap. Just make sure you do it with someone with good references. Or have a two-week vacation in an Airbnb. Just try it once and see how it feels.

You can check out *Where to Stay* here.

Unlock all the options of where to stay.

Activities.foreverfamilyforeverfree.com/destiny

CHAPTER 10

Living Abroad On A Budget.

Living abroad can be expensive if you live like a tourist. So we always recommend shopping and eating out where the locals go.

The great thing about house swapping and house sitting is that you end up shopping where the locals buy their food and eating out where the locals go out to eat.

We have seen some crazy expat communities that have the English stores. While we appreciate just as much as anyone else a jar of Branston Pickle sometimes, what amazes us is that people will go there and buy their weekly meat. They'll turn up there with a cool box. They'll spend crazy, above-the-odds amounts for English meat. Maybe I'm not so fussy, but I thought a chicken was a chicken, so why not buy local.

We witnessed a couple spend nearly a thousand pounds in the equivalent to Iceland out in Spain, in a tourist place. This is not somewhere you want to be doing your weekly shop. Is an English apple so much tastier than a Spanish one? Or an English chicken that has been shipped in and transported frozen better than a local free-range chicken in the country you are in? I understand the odd item that you cannot get everywhere, but not the basics, not for the price difference.

We eat plant-based, so maybe that makes a difference, but if you're in an expat community and you go out and eat out all the time, but you only go to the English shops, English restaurants for fish and chips, and English bars to drink Strongbow or Fosters, it is going to cost you a lot of money to live abroad. If you want to experience the real culture, the real country, the real food, you need to go to the local shops and restaurants. The local restaurants don't cost crazy money and the supermarkets charge sensible money because they're selling foods and fruits and vegetables that are in season and are local to that country. So you don't pay above the odds for them. And you'll probably find that most places are cheaper than wherever it is that you call home.

Go to the markets

The marketplace is an amazing place to shop. In Costa Rica, we were getting three giant watermelons for $2, three giant pineapples for $2. It was incredible. In Romania, we lived quite far from the next town, which had a nice restaurant that we really liked. If we'd lived closer, we would have eaten out every single day, because the cost of living was so low. We didn't, because even though it was so cheap to eat out, it was still so much cheaper to buy groceries at the supermarket and cook at home.

Where we've stayed in Spain, the markets were amazing, especially if you use the same stalls. When we got to know the locals, they would always give my kids a cheeky handful of something or a fresh banana. When something was not looking so great, or it was past its best, we'd be given handfuls of say tomatoes. We've been given handfuls of oranges, loads of free things. They were always throwing in lemons and parsley, and you get so much for your money. Even in Spain, we've been charged up to £9 to £12 for a watermelon at the supermarkets, whereas if you get to know the local shop owners, and you buy from them and buy what is in season, you can get four huge watermelons for €10. Also, when cherries were in season, they were two kilograms for €1 at the market. At Lidl's, cherries were €5 for one kilogram, so €10 euros for two kilograms, and we were picking up two kilos for €1 at the market. Incredible, incredible, incredible.

So it really does pay to shop local and do what the locals do and go to the markets. In Costa Rica, we even ate out and had hot meals at the local markets. It cost us pennies to buy the food and it tasted incredible. So get out, try something new and enjoy the local lifestyle.

Try the local food

When you're in different countries, try the new foods, try their different flavours, try the different dishes that they do. Not only is it budget friendly, but you get to experience the world, the culture, and what it is they create, why they create it, how they've create it. Our kids love trying something new.

Some people say, "A banana is a banana. It doesn't matter where you are in the world." It gets better. I have never tasted a pineapple as good as I did in Costa Rica. Oh my goodness, it has ruined pineapples for me. Because that was the best place, I've ever tried them. If you ask our kids what their favourite food experience was, it would be raspberries in France. These amazing, beautiful fruits were fresh off the plants. In Spain, we enjoyed the fresh tomatoes and the fresh oranges. The kids could not get enough of the oranges and the orange juice in Spain. So try local, get out to those local markets, get your fresh stuff there. I promise you, it's well worth it and super delicious and budget friendly.

Cook your own meals

We meet lots of people who travel and food is their biggest expense because they eat out every single day. We wanted to make this a sustainable life. You wouldn't eat out every day at home, it would be a treat every now and then. When you're creating this lifestyle, you want to do that, too. It's okay to book a place that has a kitchen and to do a weekly shop, check out the local supermarkets, and cook some food at home.

We lived in a hotel for three months, as we managed to get a great price and it was cheaper than Airbnb. Now, this was challenging. We're vegetarian anyway, and trying to create meals with limited resources, and no kitchen wasn't easy. We had a kettle, and instant mash was a favourite back then. But we were mixing it up with different styles of salads and fruits. Mashed potato and cup o' soups were our warm treats. So you can get creative and still live on a budget. Something we have seen recently, but we have not tried out yet, is cooking with an iron. There is so much you can cook using an iron – toasted sandwiches, fish, meat and eggs. So there is no reason to eat out every meal time, even if you're staying in a hotel on a budget.

Google before you go

When you're looking at the place where you're going to stay, you can also go on Google Maps and look at the local shops, and it will have photos and prices. There are also websites where you can search the cost of living in certain areas and get quite specific to the area you're going to, to get some kind of idea of what costs you are looking at. Again, we loved Costa Rica. At the place we were staying, the bananas came straight off the trees, coconuts came off the trees. Costa Rica was definitely one of our top three budget-friendly, amazing places to stay.

A feast for six for £21

When we first flew out to Romania, we'd had a couple of crazy days and our body clocks were a little bit upside down. The amazing family we were going to house sit for picked us up at the airport and took us to this beautiful restaurant on the way home. There were six of us and we were having all this amazing food and drink, which seemed to just keep coming non-stop for a couple hours. Dave and I sat there thinking, "Oh my gosh, we're going to have to cover this because we're house sitting for them."

We hadn't worked out the currency exchange rate in any way at all, so we were completely freaking out at what this was going to cost. Now, it turns out the amazing people who we were house sitting for arranged it as a treat for us. The kids asked to see the bill out of curiosity, in their currency, it came to 120 lei. So we looked at each other like, "Oh my gosh, they just spent all this money on us."

Later on, we Googled how much 120 lei was and it was just over £21. That's like $27, for six of us to eat all this food and have all these drinks. Our minds were blown. We figured with just the four of us, we could afford to eat at a nice restaurant every single day. We didn't, but we could have.

We also went to local markets in Romania. We'd spend again about 100 lei, which is about £20, and it wasn't on just a week's worth of a few things. We're talking a sack of potatoes, a sack of onions, a box of bananas. We love our fruits and veggies, and it was cold so we bought lots of veggies to make hot stews and soups. And the local shopkeepers loved it because they were like, "Wow, here come the English. They have all this money." And we were like, "Wow, look at all this food we can get for so little money." It was a beautiful trade and it opened our eyes to what's really possible. We probably lived on £20 to £30 a week in Romania.

You can check out *Living abroad on a budget* here.

Find out the cost of living before you get there.

Activities.foreverfamilyforeverfree.com/destiny

CHAPTER 11

Accessing Your Money & Bank Fees.

Before you go anywhere, you want to really do your research with your banks and your bank cards. You want one that does not charge you abroad, for example, going abroad fees for accessing your own money. You don't want to be hitting up crazy prices every time you take cash out or you spend cash. So if you can find a bank, whether it's a building society or an online bank that doesn't charge you for taking and accessing your own money, it will save you a lot of money, we use Monzo and Revolut, which offer free cash withdrawals abroad. Otherwise, these fees can really add up, especially if you're travelling full-time. It really makes a difference. And what's also really good to be aware of is that a lot of the banks actually don't charge a percentage, they charge a fee for withdrawing cash. So if your bank charges you say £5 for withdrawing money, you'll pay £5 whether you withdraw £5, £10, £20, £100 or £200. You're going to get charged the same fee, so it can be worth taking out a week's or two weeks' worth of money so that you only get charged once and you're not getting hit up with lots of fees to access your own cash, rather than just £5 here and there when you need it.

If you take out lots of cash, make sure you're not carrying it around with you, especially if you're somewhere that's a holiday or tourist destination. Put it somewhere safe while you're out and just take what you need when you need it.

Conversion fees

Not only do banks often charge you a fee when you take out your money, they often offer to convert it into the local currency for you for a small charge or a small percentage. We have found it better not to do this because otherwise you get charged twice. So if they convert it for you, you think, "Oh yeah, they're converting it for me, my bank won't hit me up." Your bank will, so you effectively get charged twice. So we find it better to not accept the conversion, get charged in our original currency because our bank is going to charge us anyway, no matter what button we press. So if you let your bank do the conversion, it will normally be at a lower conversion rate than what you'd get for your money locally and you'll get charged twice – once for taking out your money and once for the conversion into the local currency.

Expiry dates

When you are out and about travelling, it's really important to keep an eye on the expiry dates of your cards. We've been caught out with this one. Make sure you get your new card shipped out and ready to use, because once your card has been shipped out, which can take anywhere from five to 10 working days, the bank then stops the original card from working and activates the new one, assuming that you've already received it. So make sure you keep an eye on those expiry dates, and maybe have a backup. If you know you've got a card that's due to expire and you haven't got a back-up or an extra card, take out enough cash to cover you until your new card arrives. And make sure that whoever is going to be sending out your card does so as quickly as possible. We usually arrange for cards to be sent to us registered mail to make sure they get to us as soon as possible.

If you happen to have a date when you know you're going to be travelling back to your home country or your hometown, if your cards are close to their expiry, it is worth calling up your bank and saying that you've worn your card out, you've broken it, you've put it in a washing machine, and asking them to send you a new one. If you time it correctly, when you get home, you will have a new card waiting for you, rather than having to try and make it work when you're out travelling.

Accessibility

Another thing with accessing your money, if you are receiving money from clients or work, be sure you can access it or transfer it so you can get access to it wherever you are. We have global clients, so sometimes they're sending us money in US dollars, Canadian dollars, Australian dollars, euros or pounds. We get paid in all sorts of currencies. Or maybe you're just staying with people and they want you to do a transfer to cover a cost of something. You don't want to keep getting hit with lots of crazy fees.

There are some amazing online banks, online payment gateways, that either charge minimal fees or don't charge for this, and you can transfer from dollars to pounds, or pounds to Australian dollars, or Australian dollars to euros, without the hefty fees.

You can find more in the Resources section at the back of the book.

Spare cards

When things go wrong, flexibility and resourcefulness are your best life skills. So it's really important to have spare cards, and different ways to access your money. You need more than one card in case you lose your card, you break your card or your wallet gets stolen.

You can check out *Accessing your Money* here.

Where share many different options to access your funds!

Activities.foreverfamilyforeverfree.com/destiny

Part 3:

Being Prepared

CHAPTER 12

Things Do Go Wrong.

Forced to be resourceful

We've had some crazy unlucky moments. David once lost his phone on an airplane, it had his driving licence and his bank card in it. And my bank card had broken, the chip had fallen out of my card, and for some reason, the PIN on our spare bank card just wouldn't work. Even when they sent us new PINs, it wouldn't work and we were literally stranded with no way to access our cash. So we had to get super resourceful.

This happened to us while we were in America. As there was no chip in my card, the ATM wouldn't accept it. But I could take it to Bank of America, show my passport and my bank card, and they would access my funds and give me cash. So we were like, woo hoo, this gives us money, gives us time, so we can get the new cards sorted out for our next place.

When we travelled to France, it wasn't the same. I tried lots of different banks and they looked at me like I was crazy. They were like, "But you don't bank with us. No." This wasn't an issue in America. So we were shocked, stunned and stuck, to be honest.

Now, we are resourceful, so we managed to arrange accommodation and train tickets online, just using my PayPal account, which was really fortunate. We were a bit stranded, we were a bit stuck, so one night we managed to stay in a hotel. We'd booked an Ibis online and added the breakfast to make sure we were going to eat, because we'd run out of cash. It was awesome. We had a nice place to stay and a lovely breakfast. We did the cheeky thing.

We got extra bread and cheese and croissants and stuff to make a bit of a packed lunch for the kids on the train to make sure that whatever happened, they had food that day.

We were stood there waiting for the train, and jumped on, got settled into our seats and started to have lunch. Twenty minutes in, we finished and started getting ourselves ready for our stop. “Oh, not our stop, it must be the next one.” The next one came and that wasn’t it either. I was getting worried, thinking that we’d missed it whilst having lunch. We checked on Google maps and input our location. It was taking its time calibrating, so we got to the next station before we realized that we were going in the wrong direction and were heading towards Bordeaux. What we didn’t know, there’s always a lesson to be learnt, was that there were two trains two minutes apart departing from the same platform. We hadn’t noticed this, so when it called our train and said platform 2, we were at the platform ready and we got on the first train, which was not the train we wanted.

We were supposed to meet my Nan at the next train station, who was sat there waiting for us. Meanwhile, we were sat on the train heading in completely the wrong direction. We tried calling her. Unfortunately, she didn’t have her mobile with her. Bordeaux was a couple more stops away and we thought we would have more choice there than if we stopped at one of the random small village stations. We headed back in the right direction but without the correct ticket, explaining our situation to the ticket lady through my broken French. She was very helpful, and called the station to ask them to go and try and find my Nan and tell her what had happened, but they could not see her. The problem was that we were going to miss our connection, because our train was going to arrive at the station where we needed to change onto the correct line after the last connecting train for the day had left. Oh my goodness, it was so stressful.

We were desperate to see my Nan who lives in France. It was going to be awesome for the kids to see her and meet her properly, because they didn't remember her very well because they were so young the last time they'd seen her.

So again, we managed to get resourceful. We got off the train at the station where we could get the first train out the next day to see my Nan. My Nan, after waiting for us for ages, went home, called us because she had received all our messages. She wasn't feeling too good, because she had a headache, so she didn't want to drive to the station again, which was a 40-minute drive down country roads. So we booked an Airbnb that was near the train station. We tried the local taxi driver to see if he would take PayPal, which was a long shot I know, but we had no cash. As we couldn't get a taxi without cash, we left the train station and walked 25 minutes with two tired children and four cases. We got to the Airbnb about 8pm. We were ringing the doorbell, knocking at the door and not getting any response on the app, so we eventually got a number and called, "Hi, we are outside, no one is answering." The owner said, "Sorry, it's not ready yet. I was just testing to see if there would have any interest." Obviously, Airbnb would refund the £90 back, but it would take a few days.

WTF. We were like, are you kidding me? We couldn't believe our luck that day, and we were pretty much at the end of our funds. We actually had an Airbnb booked for a month that was all ready and paid for, we just couldn't physically get there and it was a beautiful place. We had enough space there for my Nan to come and stay with us. It was close enough that we could take her to the beach every day. It was going to be awesome. We just couldn't get there.

So that night we had nowhere to stay, two tired children and a train ticket for the next day. We walked back to the train station. It was warm, well-lit and it had bathrooms. We found this car hire app where you can hire people's cars, a bit like Airbnb but with cars. We thought if we can hire a car, we can drive it to our next place and wouldn't need to wait for the train the next day. I think it's called Oui car. We tried to hire a local's car rather than going through an agency because it was late and we hoped they would answer. We got through to a couple people, but then they were like, "No, it's getting late now, I can do tomorrow." We decided that we'd have to just kind of do an airport thing and sit there at the station until the morning. We got ourselves comfortable and got the coats out to cover the kids while they lay across the seats. Then the station master came over and said he was locking the train station up at 11pm. It was a small station, so it wasn't usual for it to stay open all night.

That was a punch in the face. It had been the craziest, hardest week we'd ever faced. I haven't mentioned that to get to France, we'd actually been in LAX airport for three days, because we'd bought tickets to actually fly back to London as we were due to do two speaking arrangements. So we were going to fly to London, do a few talks, see a few people and then fly over to France. When we got to the airport, they said that our flight tickets were not showing up on the system. So we tried to show them where we'd booked. We'd booked the tickets, but they hadn't come through. There was nothing we could do to speed it up, we couldn't get hold of anybody because it was a night-time flight. There was nothing they could do because we weren't on their system. They were fully booked and said we couldn't pay to get on that plane either. It had been the craziest week ever. So eventually we did get a flight, but it wasn't to London. We'd missed that weekend. We'd missed my speaking engagements. So we thought we'd fly straight to Paris, which was way further north than we were meant to be. We had a couple nights in Paris, which is where we'd spent all the cash we'd got out in America before we realized we weren't going to be able to access money in France. And we actually PayPal-ed the Airbnb host and she gave us some cash to last us the next day, when we were supposed to meet my Nan. It was all going to be great. We got the train down, stayed at the Ibis, and the next day we were supposed to see Nan.

So at this point, we were outside the station, and it had now been locked. We had nowhere to put the kids. We felt completely stuck. I have never felt as bad a mum as I did in this moment. I felt like I'd failed as a person, as a mummy, as a wife. I completely broke down. I had a complete meltdown. I was so upset and feeling so, so horrible. David stepped into his superpower in this moment and tried to calm me down, "It's going to be all right. We're going to handle this." He gave me the space I needed to have a little meltdown while he found somewhere kind of semi safe for us to just stay the night. At the back of the train station car park, there was a warehouse building which was out the way from people passing by. The last thing we wanted was for the police to come around, take our kids into care, call us the worst parents out there and have all sorts of drama going on. I waited with the kids and then we all walked through the car park with our cases, and put our stuff up against the doors on a raised platform, put extra clothes on the kids with socks on their hands as it was getting cold. It was June but still colder that I would have wanted. The kids sat on their car seats on top of their suitcases, with our coats over them. Little man was totally snuggled in on my lap, all cuddled up. I've never felt so numb sitting so still for so long. Tegan and Dave were all snuggled up trying to keep as warm as they could. I was kind of on the lookout, making sure they were okay. So I sang the kids to sleep. It was the worst night ever with my kids having to spend the night on the streets. We did downplay it and made it a bit of an adventure. We get challenges sometimes and it's not always easy. Tomorrow was going to be awesome.

The kids had seen me have my moment. They knew things weren't great. But they're really amazing kids. They didn't make a fuss. They got snuggled up and they went to sleep happy. I told Dave, "Get some sleep. I'll keep a lookout." He knew there was no way I was going to be sleeping. I had to make sure my babies were safe. What we did have was a fully charged battery pack and a mobile phone. So they all went to sleep. By this time, it was about midnight. So I got to work on my phone.

I reached out to every potential client that we had, anyone I'd been in connection with or contact with who could be a potential client, and I did not stop. And then the next morning, it was pretty much bang on 6am when I closed a deal with a client and made us $4,500, which was going to last us for a good few months. So when the kids and Dave woke up, I had this big beaming smile on my face from ear to ear, a Cheshire cat smile, and my eyes were alive and awake, even though I hadn't slept. And then it was like, but how do we access the money?

So we had all this money but didn't know how to access it. I was on a nomad Facebook group, so I mentioned about our problem of not being able to get money out and someone said "You know, you can send it to yourself via Western Union." So we managed to do a bank transfer from ourselves to ourselves with Western Union, wow how simple, but without knowing this simple trick we would have been stuck. We packed up all our stuff and walked to the Western Union office in the local town, which was a 45-minute walk away. We stopped at a park with all the suitcases and the car seats, and David sat and watched the kids, and I went on a mission to get the cash out we needed for the day, as I'd done the transfer in my name. I got quite a bit of cash out, it was probably a bit excessive, to be honest, but I was not going to have this ever happen again. We were already excited because we knew everything was going to be okay and we had a great breakfast. Because the day before we'd had breakfast at the hotel and lunch on the train, but with all the kerfuffle, we hadn't had any dinner. The plan had been to have dinner with my Nan, do a bank transfer to her for some cash, and do a week's shop and cook it at the next Airbnb.

That night, I discovered in my resourceful state – and when I say resourceful, it was when I hit rock bottom – that there's got to be another way. How can I make sure this never ever happens again? How can we have that rainy day fund? Because up to this point, we'd been travelling nearly two and a half years, and we'd paid off so much debt, which was really incredible, but what we hadn't done was pay ourselves first. We didn't have a rainy day fund. We didn't have money to fall back on. Plus the whole mix-up with losing cards, breaking cards and not having that spare bank account because we didn't know what we didn't know, had shown how vulnerable we were. From that point, we started to put a bit aside each month to keep in another account which we could use if we needed to, so that we could walk into a hotel and pay the over-the-counter prices and have somewhere to stay if we needed to.

Sitting there looking at my children thinking, how can we make sure that we never find ourselves in this situation again, I started to search "how can I live in the world for free". That's when I found there was this thing called house sitting, which was another huge game changer in our life and the way we now travel, because then it doesn't cost anything to live in all these amazing places.

So in our darkest moment also came some really great, amazing moments. And the day after was amazing. We went to see my Nan and then we went to the beautiful big Airbnb house that we'd booked with all these amazing rooms. The kids had a double bed each, we had a spare room for my Nan. She'd been feeling a bit down after losing my Grandad and she loves the beach, so we were going to take her to the beach all the time.

"You have to taste the bitter to enjoy the sweet."

I spoke with the bank about getting a new card to be shipped to us in France and they said we would need to change our address with the banks in France to get our card shipped out. So we did. This did cause problems later down the line, but we had the transcript of the chat and showed them that it was recommended by one of their customer service advisors to do it.

We were getting back on track and feeling good about things.

This was the hardest day as a parent that we went through. It was super, super tough, but it was just the start of an even greater journey.

Forced to get resourceful

Things do go wrong. Life isn't always perfect. There's so much that can go wrong. I mean, our tickets from LA to London just weren't in the system. What we didn't realise until a week later is that PayPal had emailed us asking us to confirm the transaction because it was over £1,000, but as we didn't know, the funds didn't go through; hence, we were not on the flight system.

Some people have crazy delays, flight delays, flight cancellations, double-booked hotel reservations. We've had all these different experiences with Airbnb, with the place just not existing or the owners turning us away when we got there or the place being double booked or the booking not going through. There are so many things that can go wrong, but it's best to have a backup plan or get resourceful.

This is where it's really handy to be part of an online community of digital nomads, world schoolers or house sitters, because there will always be someone who's already been through what you're facing, and you can reach out and there'll be someone who goes, "Yep, that happened to us. Do this." Because if someone hadn't told me about Western Union that day, even though I'd made all this extra money, I wouldn't have been able to access it.

Getting lost

Sometimes things do go wrong. Sometimes we do get very lost. We've kind of ingrained it in ourselves, through trying to ingrain it in the kids, that whenever something is not how it should be, all we say is, "Oh, what's magical about this?" When we went to Costa Rica, there was something happening on the road and we couldn't get through. There was loads of traffic and it was the going to be a long time. Dave saw another car turn off down this random track, he checked it out on the sat nav and was like, "This should be the way around. I bet it's a local." And we went with it. It sounds crazy, but we went with it. We couldn't see the car ahead of us anymore, but we could see the road on the phone and could see where it would meet the main road further up. Now, the people we were following had a beaten-up 4x4 and we were in a Kia Picanto, a tiny little car that could barely fit us and the suitcases. The 4x4 disappeared quite quickly, so then we were just kind of crossing our fingers and hoping, trying to zoom in on the map to see where this barely a road was taking us, when we came to a bridge. This bridge which crossed a small stream was little more than two planks of wood the width of a car. And this was Costa Rica, so this water could have had crocodiles in it. Let's be clear, if the kids weren't with us, I'd have been screaming at David. But the kids were there, so we were like, "Wow, this is magical. Look at the wilderness that we are exploring." Tyler jumped in and said, "Wow, it would be cool if we saw a crocodile." I glared at David. It was fun and games. What was cool was after we drove across this crazy bridge and we turned back onto the main road, we got past this incident on the road really quickly and we never stopped moving. Sitting in the car in the Costa Rican sun for an hour going nowhere with no air-conditioning would not have been fun, plus the car probably would have overheated. We got to our Airbnb, met the owners, put the cases in the apartment and jumped in the pool to cool off.

We get lost all the time in different ways, whether it's just walking or driving, and have all sorts of different fun adventures. The kids have many stories to share. We let the kids navigate sometimes when we're just going for a wander and searching places, and we see amazing things. We've discovered some of the best places where we were never meant to be. We have seen those fish that skim across the water. I'm not sure what they're called, but we call them flying fish, because whilst walking to the beach, we took a wrong turn and ended up at the back of a pier. We have seen monkeys swinging in the treetops because we left the foot path and headed towards an old tin shelter to see what it was. On one beach, we saw those walking trees, the trees that get up and walk towards the water. We've seen huge iguanas, beautiful buildings, huge 3D graffiti, many unexpected things. We've made so many beautiful mistakes when we've gone the wrong way. But they're never a mistake by the time we tell the story at the end the day.

If ever you're lost and feeling challenged, try and see what is magical about the experience. Why are you here? There's a reason why you went wrong. What is it? What can you see? Who do you meet? What happens? Because every time, there will always be something magical to be experienced.

You can check out *Things do go wrong* here.

Mindset is everything, how to stay positive with the magical challenge.

Activities.foreverfamilyforeverfree.com/destiny

CHAPTER 13

Find Online And Local Communities.

Like-minded people will be your saving grace. They'll help you to feel sane while the rest of the world of people you know around you will freak out and not understand your decisions. Whether this is just choosing to home school rather than send your kids off to school. Whether this is to travel during the holidays. Whether this is just to take a year out and go travelling with the kids. Or maybe doing some house swapping with other amazing families.

The people closest to us are often the ones who don't understand our decisions. It's really great to find online support and communities, and they really are out there. From homeschooling to wild schooling, to unschooling, to world schooling, to house swapping and house sitting and pet sitting, to travelling families, digital nomads, laptop lifestyle people, single mums travelling with kids, single mums creating their own online businesses, families in business together. There are amazing communities out there to be found.

Finding your tribe

Be open and share sometimes. Often strangers can be so much kinder, have more empathy and understanding, than those we love the most. We have a lot less fear of judgement of what they will say or think. So, get out there, join some of these groups, and get to know them. Add some value in the group, and then when you need something, they will answer your questions. They will step up when you need it. They'll have resources you've never even thought of.

There are lots of incredible questions that you can ask that other people just wouldn't be able to answer. For example, what is the best mobile phone SIM plan, the best phone network to go with while travelling. The people in the mobile phone stores have sales targets to hit, so they're going to show you whatever it is they need to sell you, which is not necessarily what you need. Even the most helpful person in that store won't necessarily know what it is that you need, because they're not out travelling. So you can ask the community about that. We do it with laptops. We need a laptop that does a lot of stuff and holds a lot of power but that's nice and small so we can travel with it.

David always has a slightly bigger laptop than me, but I like to have one that's little and light, and will fit in my backpack, especially if I'm going somewhere. So these are great environments and communities to go and ask those kinds of questions. You may learn about things you might not have thought of or that even people in stores wouldn't know the best answer to.

You can find a few of our recommendations in the Resources section at the back of the book.

And of course we have our own community that you can come and join. We'd love to see you there and have you share your experiences, and watch our amazing journeys, as we still continue to travel.

It really is important to have some like-minded people to be able to connect with, to watch their journeys, to be able to share your stories with, without any guilt, any pressure, any concerns about what they will think and what they will say. This really will keep you sane while the rest of the world thinks you're crazy.

On these communities, you'll find amazing advice and tips and support. Everyone's been through something crazy at some point. And your question, no matter how small or how crazy, will get seen and will get answered, by people who have lived it. Whereas if you ask those who are living in the box and not understanding your choices, their answer is always going to be to come back and do the normal thing. Someone who's been through it will have an incredible suggestion you didn't think of, or a resource you never knew about, or a community that you should get in touch with. There are always amazing ways around any issue.

I've benefitted from it too. Unfortunately, I lost two of my grandparents within five weeks of each other, and this was at a time when we still weren't doing great financially. So, when I went over for the first funeral, we literally used all the money we had that week to get me there. And as I arrived, the Airbnb cancelled. I know. Again, right? It cancelled on the day I was due to arrive. All my money was in that Airbnb. It was probably only about £27 for the night. But they cancelled on me and my money was in that, so I couldn't pay for another one, because we were literally playing it day by day.

Through the community, I found out about something called 'couch surfing'. I went onto this community and I found this amazing couch surfing app. You could do 10 free messages a day before you had to sign up, back then. I was freaking out, messaging all these people who had great response rates. I messaged all 10 saying, "I'm in the area looking for somewhere. My Airbnb's cancelled on me. I'm unable to book one for tonight."

Actually, I didn't find a couch to surf on that night. So, the night before the funeral, I felt completely alone. I was still working on my Grandad's eulogy to try and do a great job for my Mum, to make sure it was good, practise it, whilst trying to figure out what to do.

I thought, "I know. I'll go back to the airport. I'll just stay in the airport overnight, because I feel safer within an airport." I was trying to get to the airport. I couldn't even get the bus. I was like, "Do I eat or do I get the bus?" I decided to walk and eat rather than get the bus to the airport. I was walking through this big country park, following my Google maps on my phone to get to the airport, and my phone died. I had no idea where I was going. So I asked this couple walking through the park with their dog, if they could give me directions to the airport. They looked confused that I was walking this crazy distance. They asked me if I was okay. I shared how my day had been. And with it being that I was over there for a funeral, feeling so much pressure and having my accommodation cancelled, everything felt like it was going wrong. I had a mini meltdown.

I teared up trying to explain what was going on. They were a beautiful couple. This is where I really believe that all the kindness we put out there in the world serves us when we need it the most. These people were my saving grace. They were really beautiful, amazing people. They insisted that I come around for cup of tea and at least charge my phone. When they asked why I was going back to the airport, I was like, "I'm just going to stay there the night. I'd feel safer there than just somewhere on the streets by myself." They were like, "Well, the airport shuts at 11, so that plan won't work." If I hadn't met them, I would've got all the way there in the dark and had nowhere to go.

They made up their spare room for me. They insisted I join them for dinner and stay there the night. I was able to have a nice dry, warm, safe bed to sleep in. I was able to call David and tell him I was okay, and explain what had happened, and the crazy mission I'd been on. While I was there, I actually heard from one of the couch surfing people, and they were right near where my family would be staying for the night before the funeral. I agreed that I'd go to see them the next day and get myself all checked in there. This couple was amazing. They gave me their name and email on a piece of paper, but it rained and the ink ran and I lost their details, and I've never been able to get back in contact with them. If by any chance you're reading this book, *I love you. Thank you. You're amazing. It meant so much to me in that moment. I really could not ever explain.*

The next day they drove me to where this couch surfing place was. They seemed a bit worried because it was in this block of flats that didn't look too impressive, whereas they were from a really nice neighbourhood. He was like, "I'm going to wait here till you tell me it is okay." I went in and it was a bit interesting. The people were a little bit out there. But they'd opened their home to complete strangers for free just to help people travel and get around. Their open-mindedness drew me in more than the things I was seeing. I went out, I didn't want to push my luck with these other beautiful people, who I'm sure would've put me up again, but I didn't want to outstay my welcome. I thanked them very much and stayed with the couch surfers.

It was awesome, because then my family arrived, so I went and joined them at the hotel and went with them to the funeral. After the funeral, we all had dinner together, and then I headed back to my place. I'm sure they thought I was going to a hotel or an Airbnb. It wasn't until the next visit that I shared what had happened.

When I went back five weeks later, I'd had an incredible time. We'd made amazing sales that month. We'd made a year's worth of sales that month.

We'd had our most incredible month. Remember I said that whenever we get knocked down hard, we seem to get back up stronger than ever. So the bigger the setback, the better the comeback. Again, it really pushed me and gave me that drive and motivation to really make sure that that situation did not happen again.

Within five weeks, I was back again to say good-bye to my Nan. This time I was able to book a flight at a decent time of day and stay in a hotel. After that, I flew off to Vegas for an incredible event. Those two trips, just five weeks apart, were completely different. I felt like a completely different person. The first one was nothing but stress and tears and anxiety. And oh my goodness, I'd left my kids. I was asking myself, "Should I have even come?" But because I'd been asked to write and speak the eulogy, I felt that pressure. I really wanted to be there and step up to be there for my Mum.

When I went back for my Nan's funeral, it was so much more relaxed, and I didn't have to worry about what I was going to eat, where I was going to stay. My travel was all arranged. I was due to get the train up to see my sister and stay with her before I flew to Vegas. My big brother came to the funeral and actually gave me a lift up to my sister's, which was incredible, because we got all that time together. He actually asked me, "So where did you stay last time?" When I explained the kind of place I stayed in, oh my gosh, he gave me an ass-whooping. He told me off and said he would've sorted me out, which I knew he would. I'm just terrible at asking for help. Even through all this self-development that I've done, I still struggle. He then proceeded to tell my sister, who also told me off. But pride gets in the way sometimes. We're all still learning and growing. But if I hadn't found that community, I wouldn't have found the sofa surfing or house sitting.

Find Online & Local Communities

If you really want to get out there and make real connections, whether in business or socially, you need to show up with confidence and share your truths. It's great that we have shared lots of possible connections and groups with other like-minded people in these forums, but if you do not take action and make those connections happen these resources will not help.

We have featured an incredible confidence coach in our book. The amazing Caroline will help you create and perfect your introduction, or your elevator pitch. Whether you want to connect with families, couples or others in business, Caroline will help you find that inner confidence and share exactly what you need to say to get the results you want and need. We love Caroline as she has been an incredible resource and friend to us.

You can check out *Find Online Communities* here.

How to enter the room and be seen, how to really connect with others.

Activities.foreverfamilyforeverfree.com/destiny

CAROLINE ANDREW-JOHNSTONE

THE REBEL

I am a Motivational Speaker who Coaches Confidence. Unleashing the inner **REBEL** inside everyone who hears me speak.

"I saw Caroline speak at TBNS 2021. It was one of the highlights of the show for me. Caroline is authentic, passionate and motivating. She speaks from the heart, sharing experiences and lessons learned. A fabulous keynote speech to end the day on a high."

Kath Parrington-Hough – MyMasterplan

Caroline Andrew-Johnstone

"Caroline is a natural public speaker; engaging, searingly honest, sharing hard moments but not dwelling on them, not at all self pitying. There was humour aplenty and I love the way she wove in It's all about the shoes throughout. Plenty of business and life tips too. Marvellous!"

Alison Cooper - Not Just Travel

The Rebel Who Found Her Voice

I am a Yorkshire lass born and bred. Lots of things happened in the year I was born especially that England won the world cup for the first and only time. Mum was a cleaner at the Hospital and Stepdad was a miner. I came from a very working class background; these roots gave me the greatest start in life.

I am the mother of 2 fur babies. Luey and Melvin (no kids) and a wife to Christopher.

My background is sales at senior management level whether that be Sales Director or International Business Development Director.

My career started in Yorkshire but eventually led me to the Big City where I worked alongside international and national Organisations such as Reed Recruitment, Guardian Glass, Saint Gobain, Orange (EE now), British Gas, The Bank of Kuwait and First Direct.

I'm a strong believer that you keep trying until you get it right. Two failed marriages, 3rd time is a work in progress but it's getting there.

www.rebelspeaker.co.uk

CHAPTER 14

Breaking Away From The Norm.

What changed everything for us? We were at a point where we had to make a decision. Do we go bankrupt? Do we go into social government housing? Do we give up on all the ideas we had? Do we put the kids in school, both go out and get work, and try and start again? Or do we make a change? Do we do something really different, break away from the norm and create our own way?

We had one month's rent left before we were going to have to declare bankruptcy. A couple of months before this, we'd heard about this guy called Tony Robbins. He was coming to the UK in two months. It seemed too coincidental to not go for it. So, instead of paying rent that month, we thought, "We're going to lose it all anyway. Let's buy this ticket. Let's go see this person. Let's see if it really can make a shift and a difference and help us create our own way."

Wow. This was by far one of the best decisions we've ever made, and one of the biggest life changes we've made. I went and played all out. I gave my everything to this event. I put my heart and soul into it. I was so open for changes that whenever that opportunity came and arose, I took it, and I took myself as deep as I could. I went all in. This led to new ideas. When I came back, I started a morning routine. Within a few months, I'd dropped five stone. It made such a difference to my brain, to my body, to my energy. And it led to such incredible ideas. It helped me get really resourceful and realise that resourcefulness is one of my superpowers. If there isn't a way, we are going to create it. It wasn't about other people anymore, doing what we think is best for them. We needed to do what was best for us and our kids.

We started creating a plan. We worked out all our finances like we described in chapter two. What is our number? How can we change this number? Because, at the time, we were already living on a minimal amount. We didn't have a TV licence, Sky or Netflix or Amazon, gym memberships, magazine subscriptions. We didn't have anything like that. We literally had the bare basics. We were down to one car, and minimal insurance, the least we could have. Everything was as minimal as it could be. There was no way that we could change or lower our expenses anymore. We had to create a new way. We got thinking about the whole idea of Airbnb's, and we loved the fact that you can stay in one and the price includes everything except the food. You do not have to pay extra for water, gas, tax, rent, all these different things that add up to make a big price. We worked out if we could find a place for less than our number, we'd be winning. We were making a step forward.

David, at the time, worked for a big chain, a big company, and we were based in Cornwall. He looked into getting a transfer up to London. In London, his salary would increase quite dramatically because he'd be going from a little village into a big city. We were able to find a place where we could stay for a much, much reduced cost. Our expenses were going to go down, and our income was going to go up. Finally, we would almost be breaking even, or maybe be able to actually start paying things back. We had found the way. Were we brave enough to actually make it happen?

It wasn't easy. It was well thought through, but it was tough to start with.

We were taking the kids away from everything they knew and had grown up with from quite a young age. And we didn't know if it was going to work. But at this point, we looked at each other and we laughed. What's the worst that can happen? We can give up now, go get help and support from the government, get that government housing, go out and try and find jobs each, get the kids into school. That could be the way things work out, anyway. Why not risk it and take a chance? What if it does work? What if we can make this happen? Wouldn't that be something?

We'd never had a TV. We'd always had a big world map up above our fireplace where, as part of the homeschool learning fun, and we had sticky notes all over this map of places where we wanted to go, why we wanted to go there, foods we wanted to try, places we wanted to see, things we wanted to learn, languages we wanted to discover. We were always dreaming big. I'm a big picture person. Any of my clients who have worked with me will totally agree that I'm this big picture person, with these big dreams. If your dream isn't scaring you and making other people laugh at you, it is not big enough. So we dared to dream big. We burnt all the boats. We gave up our house. We gave up our cars. We gave all our stuff to those who needed it. We jumped all in, and it changed our life as we knew it. We had decided at this point that it would be more painful to not try.

We finally got to the point where it would be so much more painful to give up and settle for mediocracy, to fail and crumble, and have to start again. What if we tried this and it actually worked? What if we managed to pull this off? What if this new way we were creating was the life we were dreaming about? What if we just dared to be brave enough? Then we got far more excited by the possibilities of it. We were more motivated by what if it did work than scared about what if it didn't. So if it didn't, we were going to end up in the same place as if we didn't try.

What do you risk by not making it happen? What's the consequence of you not doing this, of you not trying? When it comes to your relationship, your connection and bonding with your children, your health, you can create life on your terms and you can make that choice right now. Equally, you can sit back and do nothing. What will that cost you? Imagine being in the same place in five years from now, 10 years from now, 20 years from now. How does that feel? That's why we went all in, that's why we burnt our boats. That's why we jumped and we have never looked back. It actually worked out for us.

David's perspective

We did jump in and we did burn our boats. I just kept my life jacket on. At the beginning, when we left to go travelling for our first flight, instead of handing in my notice, I called in sick and said, "Laura's not feeling too well and I won't be in for a few days." I made this call while I was at the airport, ready to fly and be off forever more, or that's what we hoped would work. So I called back four days later and said, "Yeah. Sorry. Still not too good. I'm going to be off a few more days. I'll see you back on Monday." By this point, I'd had a week off and this gave us the chance to see if it would work. We realized how much extra time we had that we could use to work on our own business. Before when I was working, I'd get up at seven o'clock in the morning and then I'd commute for an hour to get to work.

I'd be there working all day and finish at five o'clock. I'd then have another hour's commute, get back for six o'clock, or half six, if there was too much traffic on the road. By that point, I'd be physically and mentally exhausted.

When we had that first week, and I called in sick, we still worked on our own business and doing what we needed to do. But I had so much more energy, waking up at 7am, seeing the kids, playing games and having breakfast altogether. By 9am, I was doing work formatting a book, trying to get so much in, and by 11am we'd go to the beach and have fun until lunch. It was so nice sitting down enjoying lunch together as a family. After lunch, I'd get a couple more hours of work in. Then I'd manage to

read a story to my children, as it had been many months since the last time I'd read to them. I played with the kids during the day, but it wasn't so mentally exhausting. We did stuff that we needed to do. And after the kids had gone to bed, we could just work, work, work, and we were like, "Wow, we got so much more done." After that week, I realized what we were going to be able to do this.

So I called up my boss on the Monday and said, "I'm going to be off for a few more weeks. I need a bit more time." After three months, my boss called me up and said, "Okay, no problem. I take it you're not going to come back for now. If you ever want to come back, not a problem, come back. And it's fine. Just take what time you need."

So he gave me that reassurance that I was not dropping him in the shit anymore. But he knew that I was not coming back, but the offer was still there. He was a great boss. So I still kept a pinkie in. I didn't really want to quit there. And six years later, I still haven't actually quit. My toolbox is still in that garage.

Instead of spending the day doing something I didn't enjoy away from the people I loved, I was getting truly filled up every day. Seeing my kids laugh and play and doing amazing things together filled me up. It recharged me. So I was overflowing. And by the time we'd snuggled up, read stories and they'd gone to sleep, I was so ready to put my all in, to make this be our life, to create this lifestyle, to make this happen and to make it work. I had so much more drive, determination and energy, because I wasn't out there working for someone else's dream. I was now working on my own and already seeing the results with my family and with my children.

You can check out *Breaking away from the norm* here.

What if you don't make the change?

Activities.foreverfamilyforeverfree.com/destiny

CHAPTER 15

The Scariest Train Ride

We had to get to know our numbers. We didn't have the cheat sheet we mentioned in chapter two. We had to try and figure it all out and gather all our costs together. We had to figure out what Airbnb's there were and how to do it. We didn't know then that booking by the month is actually how you saved the big bucks. This was all a learning curve for us and about playing around with the different apps. We also took a few months to clear the house and we did so many charity shop runs. We gave so much away. At Christmas, we gave so many toys and bikes and amazing things away to families in need. It was really incredible. We sold the car and had to get a taxi to the train station the day we left. It did take us a few months to get ourselves ready to start this journey.

We still had to do our research. From the first idea of doing this at Tony Robbins' Unleash the Power Within workshop to getting on our first plane took 11 months.

To start with, we left our house. We got a taxi to the train station and it was the scariest train ride I have ever been on. Cornwall to London. This is it. Boats officially burnt, we sat on a train with our children, technically homeless, creatively homeless, feeling all those feelings. No one understood what we were going through in that moment. We'd lost all our family, all our support network. We felt we'd lost so much due to our choices, but we knew it was for the best.

We knew it was going to be better for us and our children. Not only did we stay strong, but we grew stronger together. We knew it was best. We got to watch our children flourishing in these new, amazing experiences out there, living, learning from real life. They are incredible, open-minded, grounded little people and we are so proud of them. And we are so proud of ourselves for stepping up to be the best parents we can be. Doing what we believe is best for our children. None of us knows what we're *really* doing, there's no handbook on how to raise the best, brilliant child. All we can do is give them the freedom and the love to allow them to truly be themselves and get out there and make a difference.

And from that train journey, when we first got to London, we then spent another eight months working in London, building up some bank, because we were screwed at the beginning. We needed some money and we saved money from having this extra pay with the job transfer and lower expenses with Airbnb. So that gave us another eight months of travelling around, also trimming down our bags. When we got on that train to London, we had six carry-on suitcases and six backpacks and probably a couple of carrier bags as well. We needed to trim down even more. So each time we moved, and we moved eight times while we were in London, we realized that if we had not used an item for a month, we probably didn't need it. So we still kept it until the next move, and if we hadn't used it by that move, it went either to the charity shop or in the bin. If we didn't need it, we weren't going to keep it. So during that time, we really trimmed our bags down to what we actually used and just kept what we needed.

CHAPTER 16

Finding Life Balance.

How do you create balance and happiness? This choice is ultimately yours, and only you can make it. We purposely live a life by design so we can enjoy our kids now. David used to work and be up before the kids and be back by the time they were in bed. This was not great for family life. We used to let the kids stay up a little later just to get an hour's playtime with Daddy before they went to bed, because we wanted to create that bond. When we purposely changed our lives to make it by our design, we wanted it so that we get to play all day with the kids. Then, in the evenings, when they go to sleep, that's when we get our laptops and devices out, and we go crush our business.

Sometimes, there's the odd event or scheduled call or meeting that comes up in the day. But generally we get to play with our kids every day. And in the evenings, four or five nights a week, we're crushing our business. Because it is also important to have your date night or your couple time. But this is a choice only you can make. If we'd left the kids in school and gone full pelt on our business, our business would be huge by now, we'd be smashing the numbers. Money would not be an issue, and we'd be absolutely rocking and rolling. But by the time we'd hit this success, our kids would've grown so much. We would've missed out on so much. You can crush business and relax later. It depends what it is you want. If you don't have kids, go crush it while you have time. You have no idea the abundance of time you have until you've had a child and suddenly it's gone. If you have an abundance of time, energy and resources, go out there, crush it. Crush it so big and so hard. Work for the next two years like you've never worked in your life, so you never have to do that again. Because once you get to that tipping point, then the whole game changes.

Shifting Focus

With our children, we learn and we grow together. We don't think we have to know everything to be able to teach it to our kids. We laugh at each other, especially with languages. The kids are always better than the grown-ups. They pick languages up so much faster, because they do it through fun and play. They really do. They're like, "We'll go to the shop." And it's like, "Mummy, I got this." And they do. They handle it way better than me. We grow, we learn, we do a lot of things together. The daytimes are so special.

I always thought I helped Dave create an amazing bond with our children, because on the weekends he would have them for that first hour of the morning if he had any of the weekend off, so I could catch up on sleep. And in the evenings, the kids would have an extra hour, stay up later than they should be really, to get that quality time with Daddy. That first month that he didn't go to work and we started creating this lifestyle, it was a whole new level of bonding. I wouldn't have believed the difference if I hadn't seen it with my own eyes. There was a completely different level of bonding and connection. It was truly magical. It was worth every struggle we'd ever been through to just have that bond that we'd created.

When they're at school and you're at work, you miss out on so many amazing things. You miss out on them learning and growing and discovering. You miss out on those quality meal times when you sit and you discuss and talk about your day and what you've learnt or achieved or seen that day. We really value our family meal times.

Gratitude exercise

A habit that we got into very early on was in the evenings we would take a sheet of paper and write three amazing things that had happened that day, something we were really grateful for, and something we really loved that someone else did for us in the family, and three things we were going to achieve the next day. It just became the thing that we do all the time. Now we don't even need the sheet of paper, it's just something we can just discuss and have a real giggle about.

Be Present

When it comes to work-life balance, so many parents are out there getting very stressed because they're trying to do everything at once. One of the key things that we teach when we're talking to parents who are overwhelmed is to do one thing at a time. This sounds so simple, but it's so overlooked. So many people try to work whilst entertaining the kids. You can't do it. There's no focus. If you go and take an hour of time for yourself, especially if you're a couple, if mum or dad goes and takes an hour for themselves, they can go and crush what they need to get done, with 100% focus and concentration. You are going to achieve so much more in that one focused hour than you would of four hours of trying to balance work and play.

Equally, when you're with the children, be present, be with your children. It will make a huge difference in your connection, in your bonding, of them knowing that you are showing up and you're being there for them, of you really listening and taking in what they have to say. Then, when you go do the work, it doesn't affect them as much, because when you're there with them, you're fully there. They're not fighting for your attention because when you're present, you're present. As I mentioned at the beginning, if you are a couple, also make sure you get that quality couple time.

If, at the moment, you're still trying to create the funds to start changing your lifestyle and you are working more, it can still happen. Just as you schedule the odd appointment to the dentist or the doctor, schedule in your family time. Make sure you make time to develop and maintain those bonds, those connections.

In our first book, we go into this in more detail and explain the three steps to family that we created (realign, reconnect, grow together). We recommend going and checking it out. There are printed and audio versions of the book. So, if you are commuting to and from work, you can just listen to it in the car. There are no bad words, so you can even listen to it with the kids around.

You can check out *Finding Life Balance* here.

Design it your way! No right or wrong… Only right for you!

Activities.foreverfamilyforeverfree.com/destiny

CHAPTER 17

Home Is Where The Heart Is

"Sometimes a home isn't four walls.

It's two arms and a heartbeat."

First, I want to start with our definition of home. Our kids know where they come from, but we believe home is where we all are together. Basically, home is where the love is. Your definition of home is whatever you define it to be. If you have given up everything, or you're deciding to go that way, it could be the new camper van that you call home. It could be Granny's house, because whenever we go back to our country, we go stay with Granny. You decide what is home to you. Remember, if you choose a camper van as your home, and the camper ever breaks down and you've got to replace it, you've attached home to a thing. We very much believe that home is not a place, it's that feeling of love and safety for our children. And they really understand that.

In the beginning of our journey, when our little boy was four years old, to him, home was where Ted bear was, his special teddy. Even when we were out in some crazy gazebo somewhere sleeping in a hammock, home was where Ted bear was. Even before we started travelling, before we gave up our home, when we would go away for a few nights and stay in a hotel, whether it was in London doing an event or up seeing family, when we were out for the day and we'd go, "Okay, time to go home", the kids knew where we were going to sleep that night. They knew we were just popping back to the hotel. And when we'd pack our bags at the hotel and pack up the car, and say, "Okay, we're heading home now", they knew we were returning to the house we were living in. They just knew, even before we started this lifestyle, that home is where we are sleeping that day. Home is where we're going to be all together.

So it's never been anything they've got stuck on. I know some people are distraught when, in their adulthood, their parents sell their childhood home. It's where they grew up. We've never really had that attachment. We really believe, as the saying goes, that home is where the heart is, and our hearts are all together, so that's where our home is. Maybe you can start by taking a look at what home is to you. What makes a house a home? Because where you live is just a building. What is it that makes it a home?

Stability for the kids

This is a big thing that the people who loved us threw at us in the early days. What about stability for the children? David and I are their stability. We're a really solid couple. We're a solid foundation. We didn't even have children until we'd been together for 10 years. We didn't take the decision to have kids lightly, and we are here for them. We love them, and we're here together. So their stability is us and our family unit.

This got questioned so much in the early days. When we look at the people around us who we love and care about, and even us as kids, we've both had parents who have divorced, and you're between your mum's house, your dad's house. If something happened one weekend and they're busy, then you're off to Grandma's house. That's not stability either, being shared and pushed and pulled here and there. There are lots of situations out there where one parent is trying to come and pick up the kid, and then the other parent doesn't let them. That is not stability, when they're not able to see their kids. It's not necessarily through anyone's fault, but sometimes we feel that is a lot less stability than what we give our children. That's our perspective. And that's not us judging anybody, but people used to really go for us on that one, "What about the stability for your kids?" We are that. We are a solid unit. They know they've got us no matter what. Our family, us as a couple, is the stability our kids have no matter where we are on the planet.

You can check out *What is Home to You* here.

Watch the video and have that important conversation!

Activities.foreverfamilyforeverfree.com/destiny

CHAPTER 18

Handling Judgement.

This is one of those "it's easier said than done" pieces of advice, because it is tough. Even when we'd just started homeschooling, some people crossed the street and de-friended us on social media because that was too far out the box for them. Can you imagine how they felt when we gave up our house, all our belongings, had just a carry-on case each and started travelling the globe? People thought we were crazy. This lifestyle was not well heard off and wasn't a cool thing when we started this journey, and people thought we were nuts. People threatened to call social services on us, thinking our kids weren't safe, which really shocked us because if anyone knows us for longer than five minutes, they know we are all about our children.

So this can be tough and it will be the people closest to you, those you love the most, who will judge the most. The important thing to remember is you are a mirror, everything they're saying to you and projecting on to you reflects their fears. It's the reasons why they're not doing it. And for some people, it's just too out of the box. They've been so conditioned by society. It's their way of loving you. It doesn't feel like it, I know, but it's their way of loving you and trying to keep you safe and keep you in a bubble that they understand. But you need to stay in your lane, you need to know what your why is, and remember and focus on your why. And when it comes to your children, you do know best, so stop doubting yourself. You are an incredible parent. You're doing it for the right reasons so don't let doubt creep in.

I want to stress that this can be hard. One of my bestest friends forever is my closest family member, it's my little sister, and most of our family pretty much didn't talk to us very much for almost two years. This broke my heart, completely. It didn't stop me. We still went out there. We made a difference, to see how our kids responded and grew. We weren't surviving anymore, we were thriving and it was incredible, but I always had that little niggle, and out of everybody, I really, really missed my baby sister. It broke my heart not to be sharing all these amazing experiences with her and to think of her but not be able to just pick up the phone and say, "Look, we're doing this." And have her excited for us, rather than just annoyed at us.

There was kind of a turning point where I saw a glimpse of hope. Just by staying on our track, staying in our lane, I knew the good ones would come back. Those worthy of sharing your journey would come back. We were in Costa Rica, and it had been probably for just over a year that we'd been doing all this crazy travelling and we were sharing on social media. We wanted to share our journey and show that we could go from complete lack to complete abundance.

I did a video sharing my why, why we do this, what we're doing for the kids, how and why, and some of the things we'd gone through. One of my uncles actually commented on my video. He and his wife are schoolteachers, so if you want to talk about boxes, they're neatly in their boxes. He commented, "I wish I could do for my kids what you've done for yours." I literally burst into tears.

I still don't hear from this side of the family and that used to really upset me. But that message meant so much to me in that moment. What was funny is that people kind of assumed that because my kids didn't go to school, they weren't doing the traditional things, like tv and computer games. They were expecting them to be, I don't know, maybe dumb mutes, that my kids were going to be proper little weirdos, right? Because they don't go to school, they can't socialise, yet my kids are out there playing in different languages, in different cultures, in different countries. There aren't any language barriers when it comes to play. And when they're learning through play and through fun, they pick up the words so much faster, because they want to play with the local kids.

There was a little girl in Costa Rica who my kids befriended. I never realised until then how much I say, "Good job" when my kids do something well. It was the first phrase that she started saying to everybody. My kids would jump in the pool and she'd be there, saying "Good job". And my kids learnt really quickly how to say, "Do you want to come to the pool?" in Spanish, because it's what they wanted to do. They'd sit there in the afternoons and colour in together and talk about the colours in each other's languages and learn the different colours that they were playing with. They were teaching as well as learning.

It truly was magical, but I really did struggle with that loss of contact with my closest friends and family. We only really had my Dad and Dave's little brother. They did not necessarily understand our choices and they might not have even agreed with our choices at the time, but they supported us and our decision and still stayed in touch. They still checked in. They wanted updates. They enjoyed seeing the photos. They still talked to the kids and still had that connection and closeness with us and the kids, which was pure magic, and we are so grateful for that.

A phrase I love is "What other people think of you is none of your business." It's from one of our authors actually, Anna Garcia, who does these amazing seminars and she gets the ladies to say it out loud. As I said at the start of the chapter, this is way easier said than done. We are now at a point where it's not that we don't care, but that it doesn't hurt anymore when people think we're crazy, we're making crazy decisions, we're doing nutty things. We just think, "Yeah, okay, that's fine. We still love you anyway." We don't have to agree with everybody to still love them. We're very open to that. We know it's their projections and most of it is nothing even to do with us.

Lots of people do envy our lifestyle and some people will come out and go, "Oh my gosh, you're so lucky. I wish I could live like that." Other people will just rip it to pieces and try and find fault with our lifestyle and say, "Are you sure it's right for the kids?" They'll try and find problems to make them feel better about not achieving their dreams. You really need to remember your why and know that you are doing what you know is best for you.

On our toughest days, because even we have wobbles occasionally, I'll think, "Is this the right thing for the kids?" That'll be the day that they then go and do something incredible or they'll come out with something that I didn't even know. It will just be an amazing moment, and it's almost like they're guiding us and going, "You got this. You're doing the right thing." Or the universe, whatever you believe, will just show us that little sign. It'll be a day when we receive a note from someone that says, "Your daughter's videos, your daughter's books, or something you shared, has made a real difference and a real impact, or saved a life or helped a kid." Those moments come through when we're having our toughest days. So we really enjoy that and we purposely look at that as a sign to keep on going and keep moving forward.

We did go back to the UK two years after starting full-time travel. I don't know what friends and family were expecting my kids to be like. We didn't try and do anything like "I told you so", but it was so awesome. We just went with open hearts, open minds and said hi to everybody, and they would be chatting to the kids and the kids were like, "Wow, I went to the Grand Canyon. I saw monkeys in the trees and I held an alligator." They'd had all these amazing life experiences. "Look, I can count to 10 in this many languages." They had so much great stuff to say and they're such great little people and they can hold a conversation with pretty much anyone of any age because they are naturally socialised, not ordered to conform within just their age group, so they're really amazingly sociable kids.

They've already seen parts of the world that some people have never been able to explore or get to, and I think that really opened up a lot of our friends and family to say, "There may be something to this." The biggest and most amazing thing for me was when my little sister got pregnant and during her pregnancy, we started connecting and getting closer. I was so happy and excited to have a little one of her running around. And her little girl is just like her, it's amazing. I felt like she started to understand a lot more about why we do the things we do or the way we look at things, which includes even simple things like sugar.

"No, no, the kids would rather have a piece of fruit."

"Oh, you're such a mean mum. You don't even let them watch TV."

"That's because they'd rather be outdoors."

Then suddenly, she was responsible for her own little human. I guess it just helped change her perspective, and I felt like we got super, super closer when I was able to advise her as another mum she knew who could help her with the little things that new mums worry about. New mums freak out about everything, so it's really nice to have someone else who's a mum and who's been through it just to kind of steady your nerves a lot of the time and just say, "No, no, that's okay. This is normal. Have you tried this? Have you tried that?"

I was really lucky when I got pregnant. I was nannying for an amazing lady with two beautiful girls and she was that person for me. I was able to go, "Oh, this has happened" and she'd say, "Oh, that's okay. Just do this." So my sister and I kind of got our relationship back with that.

Seeing the kids doing all these amazing things has reassured our family, and since then, they've even been out to visit us at the places we've stayed and that's been really magical. Dave's family has been out on several occasions to several different places. Dave's Mum actually came out and joined us for a month, but ended up staying six weeks because we booked her flight a bit later to go back as she wanted to stay, and we took her on a proper tour of how we lived. So for the first two weeks, she never even unpacked her suitcase.

Long story short, David booked her tickets from the completely other side of Spain from where we were, and I'm like, "We are not doing all that driving in one day." So we hired a better car than what we had. We drove and picked her up. We stayed somewhere near the airport, a beautiful penthouse suite with a jacuzzi on the roof. It was really beautiful. We took her over to Gibraltar and spent a few days over there. We got to see the monkeys on the rock and all those incredible things. We stayed in Granada with her. Again, we had this amazing apartment. We had paella up on the roof-top patio. It had a pool. It just was an amazing experience. We took her to all these amazing cities around Spain and then she spent some time with us at the base we had where we were house sitting.

It was so incredible, and I've never been closer to her than I was then. And David and I had been together for more than 10 years at this point, and I felt like she'd only just got to know us. She kind of got a sneak peek into our lifestyle and how we lived, and she fell in love with it. She thought it was great. She thought what we do with the kids is fabulous. And the more they come out and experience our life, I think the more they kind of understand us and get to enjoy the benefits, right? Because they get to come and see us where we are, visit different countries at low cost because we're already out there. They just need to get their flights. So now our lifestyle has become a bit of a bonus to them.

As I said before, we wanted to create a life that we didn't need a vacation from. That's what we've created. And I feel like we've achieved it. We're in our sixth year now and people are really finally starting to get it to the point that they're now asking a lot more questions.

<u>*David's perspective*</u>

> *So I was quite lucky with this because I didn't really have many friends growing up, so I never missed anyone or had anyone to think any differently of me. I have one good friend and if we're ever back in the UK, we meet up for a couple drinks and it's just like old times. We chat and he says where he's been working and what he's been doing, and it's pretty much always the same thing. He's hung a door in his living room, put some decking up, or something like that. And then I'll come back with, not meaning to but I'll sort of have most of the conversation, saying we were doing this, doing that, exploring different places and adventures, showing him pictures. He's fascinated, asking more and more questions about how we do it, and so I always say, "If you ever want to come out, please, please do." He would love to do what we do, but he values security so much more, knowing what is coming in each month, knowing that everything will be there when he needs it, and I totally understand that. We have a great relationship where we both respect each other's decision, and there is no "my view is right so your's must be wrong", there is none of that. I like variation, I would find doing the same thing all the time boring.*

We built this lifestyle for a reason – to connect more as a family and have fun on our terms. But it's always nice catching up because we just hit it off again and it could be a year at a time, two years at a time, until we see each other. And we're not really that connected on Facebook, so it's always nice to have a catch-up in person, and chat about everything and how everything goes on.

In terms of my family, I talk to my Dad once a month and my Mum once a month, and it's normally Laura who calls up and pranks my Dad and gives him a missed call and a call back, and says, "Hi, how are you doing?"

"Oh, hello. How are you doing?" Not knowing that she's done that.

So we've always kept in touch and we're on the phone for an hour at a time, explaining different things that the kids have been up to.

It's just so much harder, because they're stuck doing the same thing day in, day out, week in, week out. It's hard having a one-sided conversation where I talk, explain what we're doing, how we're doing it, and why. And they are doing the same thing. I chat with my little brother probably every week for an hour at a time. He has supported our life all along. He doesn't quite always understand it, but he's always there and calls the kids, and chats with the kids and asks how they're doing, and they're blown away. He was there from the beginning so he knows what they were like. He loves them as little people. So he has come out to a couple different places we've been at, and it's nice for him to see what we're doing and for us to share this with him.

Social media

What's really amazing is that we share on our social media where we are, what we're up to. I used to do a lot of live chats, but David is a bit more of an introvert and doesn't really like doing lives. So I would just get it all ready, set it up, and then go, "David?"

He'd be like, "What?"

I'd be like, "One, two, three."

He'd look at me really mad and then the camera would be on, and I'd be like, "Hey."

He'd have no choice but to join in. Once he's on, he's fine and he's himself. Because I did this so often and we were in hot places like Costa Rica, he always had his top off, which was funny because you never know who's watching. We started having people comment like, "Dave, get a shirt on, dude. You're always topless."

As I said, you never know who's actually watching. Just because they're not liking, they're not commenting or responding, doesn't mean they're not watching, and they're not loving what you're doing. I feel like us being out there, totally crazily out there, out of the box, living life on our terms, doing what we love most, doing what we do for our kids, I'm hoping that gives other families permission to get a little bit out there, to step out of their comfort zone and their box just a little and improve their life and go a little bit more crazy.

> *In this chapter, we talk a lot about other people and their negativity towards people who are doing things differently. So many people say unkind and unsupportive things when all we are doing is trying to improve our lives. It comes from a place of caring but is not helpful. During these times, it is super important for you and your family to listen to positivity and learn how to focus on the positives, as some days will be tough. Staying focused on the good has got us through many a challenge. In our resources section, we share the details of the incredible Judi-Judicorn, who is the lady of positivity, and who truly walks her talk! She is so consistent in her positivity and has an incredible workshop just for families. She has been an amazing resource and a great friend.*

You can check out What others will say & *Judgement* here.

Watch this video and set yourself free!

Activities.foreverfamilyforeverfree.com/destiny

CHAPTER 19

What Our Family Really Thought

This was interesting even for us to hear. We have not seen eye to eye with many of our family members on this journey. Yet, we still believe this has been the best thing for us and many of them have come around over time. We thought this may be of interest to you the reader as you start your own journey and come up against those who love you most.

First up is Laura's Mum. Our lifestyle is definitely out of my Mum's comfort zone, as my Mum's top value is security. What is also funny is I get my drive and determination from my Mum. She has faced many a challenge that could have beaten her, yet she always found a way to overcome them, and just like me, her strongest driving force has always been her children. So, I owe most of my bravery to her example, yet she struggles most to see us embrace these changes.

What did you think when you first heard our plans?

*When I first heard what you were doing, I was astounded. You had just adopted this lovely little girl who needed roots, grounding and stability, you had a little boy who was so young. What were you thinking? Giving everything up that they had? Admittedly, I had no idea that you did not have money and were close to bankruptcy, you always seemed to be doing so well. I thought you were f*****g crazy. And I was scared about how you and the children would cope. Would the children be okay without the stability of a boxed life?*

What were your thoughts when we in fact gave everything up and flew off?

The same. I was scared. Thought you were crazy, and I was scared for the children. Not so much about you two, because you are big enough to look after yourselves. I was just worried about everything. You suddenly just disappeared. No forwarding address, nothing. I would get the odd message that Tegan was on stage reliving her past repeatedly. I felt that this was wrong and unfair on her. However, she appeared to thrive on it, gained confidence, and blossomed. Your son started to blossom too authoring his own books and inventing things. I found it hard to communicate with both without criticising you. I have been so poor that I have gone without so that my children could eat, times were so hard, I worked hard to give them everything and was scared that they would suffer too. Every time we would talk, you were so evasive about things, I worried that the children would come to harm at all these strangers' houses they were staying in. You became vegetarians. Children need milk and meat. I felt that they should be able to make their own decisions about what they eat when they are old enough. I worried, that is what parents / grandparents do. It was easier and less harmful not talking to you, as it was hard not to argue. What about the children's schooling, what about when they are old enough to leave the nest? What qualifications would they have? Are you all mad?

What are your thoughts now, six years later?

Over the years, I have mellowed, I have seen that the children have not suffered, your family is happy and that is the most important thing of all. All I ever wanted was for your happiness. Do I still think that you are crazy? YES. Does it matter? NO. I just suppress the instinct to be critical and I try to be there if you need me. No more judgements, I am just at that stage where I do not want to lose you. Live and let live. I still don't agree with the fact that the children haven't got any of what I call proper structure, boxed structure should I say, as you use the word so well. Yes, it's exciting, but I do feel having no roots can cause underlying problems.

I think you are crazy, but I'm just glad that you are happy as I said before. I still think you are all absolute nutters, and I could not live with the stress of not knowing where the next penny is coming from. Or where I'm living next.

I can see Tyler being like Bear Grylls in the future.

What would stop you from doing this lifestyle?

Security, knowing where the next meal's coming from. Not knowing where the next penny's coming from, that is what I'd be worried about. In a way, I almost envy your freedom and courage, I wish that I could do that. I have worked since I was fourteen, I have always been the breadwinner of the family, life has been hard and still is, I wish that I too could survive like you do, but there is too much fear within me. The box that surrounds me, that is ingrained in me is made of steel and keeps me in my current situation.

WENDY HELEN – Laura's Mum

Next up is David's little brother Carl. He moved to Cornwall and lived with us for about a year, six months, at the same time as my Dad was living with us. David used to joke that we should call our house "Herbies Hostels". He moved out and we had a plan to move. He was incredibly close to Tyler and Tegan and has seen them grow over the years. He has been the most supportive over the years. He has not always understood, but has always been happy for us. Hearing him tell us that we left him there in Cornwall was hard to hear as we thought he was settled and never gave him a thought. We are sorry, Carl. Carl was one of the only family members who fully supported us. His love and support were a big part of our drive to push forward in tough times. He was our no. 1 fan and we Love him SO much.x.

What did you think when you first heard our plans?

You were crazy. You were willing to do anything you could to get where you want. I believed you would never stop trying. The first few business opportunities you tried, you failed. I thought that you were just chasing dreams. You could be like me, don't try and be nothing. Or you keep on doing it, keep on trying and one day you'll succeed. And you have.

You were there the day we left, so what were your thoughts when we in fact gave everything up and got on the train?

*You f*****g left me in Cornwall when you brought me down here. I was like, "You b*****d!" Only kidding, my first thought was how much I'm going to miss you. I saw you off from the house. Yeah, I was going to miss you. I wanted you to succeed in your adventure so much. Whether it was going to work or not, I didn't know, I couldn't judge it. I don't think I could have done it. Technically, you weren't leaving anything behind. You were free in something new. It was a challenge and I think you were f*****g crazy doing it. But you were brave. You had the balls to stick through it and no matter what hurdle you had, you just kept doing it and not giving up. Yeah, you never gave up. Not even when you did hit rock bottom and you had nothing. You didn't give up.*

I think you lost quite a bit of money and time from your other business opportunities. I think you failed quite badly many times. But then that was it, the next day you were trying something new. I was thinking, "What?" And watching you, then you got me into it. I gave up as soon as I lost money. Trying to sell stuff on Amazon. I thought, "This is costing me more money than I am actually making." But I didn't give it up completely there, I was just much more wary, I copied. Kept going a bit, I should have kept on going, but I didn't. You two, you have kept going and you haven't stopped since and look at where you are now.

What are your thoughts now, six years later?

Nothing and no one has any hold over you, that is amazing, and I love that! You have created life so you can do whatever you want, whenever you want. Nobody asks you for any money, rent, electric, water, gas, TV, jobs. You're very self-sufficient.

As for the children, you look at them now and they are switched on. They've got common sense. They have grown up. They have matured. They are so free, very creative and very loving. If I had a child now, and it was my responsibility, I would not put my children into school or into the system. Not one bit.

I saw Tegan when she was in school. She got bullied so bad and you had all that trouble with her teachers, but then you took her out. At first, I was thinking, "What?", but with what I know now is that if I had the responsibility, I would not put my children in school. I think Tyler was a bit shy speaking but now he certainly is not. They have both absolutely thrived. I don't know any children that go to school and have written books like Tegan and so many books from Tyler, that have created board games and inventions, that have been up on stage, walked on glass, walked on fire, broken through wooden boards, that is such a powerful lesson overcoming their fears. I don't know any others that have ever done that. Or would even try or even think about trying that. They've had a completely different experience and it's been worthwhile without a doubt. They haven't missed out on anything; they have gained so many incredible life experiences.

How do you feel when you come visit our crazy lifestyle?

Comfortable. If I could get a job right here right now on the computer selling something, I would do it, straight away. I don't know, I've been looking, and I've been thinking so hard. It's like, "Oh, come on, there is something out there." I just need to keep on thinking. I would do it in the blink of eye. I'd just give up everything for that sort of lifestyle. It's different with me though. I would have to have a permanent home. I couldn't be living, not knowing where I was going to be next. I don't like that fear. But that's me. Crikey, how many countries have you all been to? How many exciting things have you all seen? How have they been influenced by all these countries?

And thinking of the future, where do you think our kids will be ten years from now?

Ten years from now, knowing your children, they'd most probably own Mars. Or probably the sun, you wouldn't go for a planet, you'd go for the sun. I believe Tyler will own a sort of nature reserve place, woodland place. Rescuing all the animals and keeping them all. Living out in the wild in luxury. With no worries. Still be living that lifestyle, living in the middle of nowhere. He most probably would have electric there, but he would still be building his own fires, I know he would.

Tegan, ten in years' time, I don't know. Now heading through these teenage years, she has the chance to create any possible future, whatever she wants to achieve I believe she will do it.

What would stop you from doing this lifestyle?

Certainty. Certainty. I like certainty. I like to know where my next pay cheque is coming from. I like to know where I'm sleeping that night. Yeah, that would be my biggest thing, certainty. If I knew I had a bit of money in the bank, and got out of debt, and only earning a little bit. If I knew I was guaranteed to earn a little bit each time, each month. It wouldn't have to be millions, but something so that I know I've got a little bit coming in each month, just to cover where I'm living and what I'm eating. I'd be fine. But, giving up everything, if you didn't have a job, you didn't have anything, just got on a plane, and just got out there. I don't know that I could do that. I don't think my heart rate would keep up with that.

I don't know if you have shared this, but you have faced a lot of negativities. You had so much negativity about your choices, from everyone, your friends, your family, and despite all that, you still went on and did it. Yeah, you just proved them all wrong. You have lost a lot of family over the time. Okay, you have rebuilt quite a bit now, but you did lose quite a bit along the way, which must have been extremely hard. But you never gave up, and you just proved that you're right.

CARL HERBERT – David's Brother

Now we have Yvonne, David's Mum. We only really saw eye to eye when she came out on holiday with us for six weeks. For the first week, she travelled around with us and got to see the adventures and the life that we lived. Seeing us in person and how we are with the children, she got to know us for real.

What did you think when you first heard our plans?

You have done more than most. Your children have seen more than most. I would have loved to have done what you all have done. What a wonderful life the family has.

I think they're brilliant. I think it's a wonderful way to see the world. And, as I've said, the family has in fact seen more than anybody, than most people ever see in their lifetime. You've experienced different cultures.

What were your thoughts when we in fact gave everything up and flew off?

Brilliant. Brilliant. I would have loved to have had your life.

I travelled with you and lived your lifestyle for a little bit. I thought it was brilliant. The only thing I didn't like is the food you eat. Because I'm not a vegetarian. But that's the only thing. But going about everywhere, living out of my suitcase was brilliant. I had a fantastic holiday.

Your children have seen things I will never see in my lifetime. When they get older and put it all together, you will find, they're going to be brilliant grown-ups.

And thinking of the future, where do you think our kids will be ten years from now?

Oh, that is a hard one. I'm not quite sure about Tegan, in some ways, she will achieve whatever she sets out to do.

Tyler, I think he will write more. I think he will put more into perspective when he gets older into a book of all the life, from his view. Of a child's view, not a grown-up's view.

What would stop you from doing this lifestyle?

The problem is that I couldn't do that. I'd never be able to afford insurance for myself. Because I'm diabetic. Insulin is very, very expensive. I know I could never do it. But if I wasn't a diabetic, then yes. If I had known about this house sitting years ago, I would have probably done something about it.

And you've done it in all different countries. Brilliant.

YVONNE COOPER – David's Mum

Mikey is a Laura's younger brother. We love him to pieces though he has never been the best at staying in touch. We always pop in and say hi when we are in the UK, and he is the proud dad of three awesome children. It was great to have him share his thoughts with us.

What did you think when you first heard our plans?

When you first shared your crazy idea, I thought there's a lot to see and learn, have fun but please be safe.

What were your thoughts when we in fact gave everything up and flew off?

Wow, how brave! I wish I was that adventurous.

What are your thoughts now, six years later?

Six years on, you guys have worked hard to create happy memories and have many great stories to share.

Where do you see the children ten years from now?

I believe your kids will still be adventurous and seeing even more of the world, maybe with friends or partners of their own. They will have so many great adventures and stories to share.

What would stop you from doing this lifestyle?

I couldn't just up and leave everything, as much as I would love to. My kids are everything to me and they are happy in their lives as they are, and I want to be around to watch them grow up.

MIKEY HEDLEY – Laura's Brother

Derek, David's Dad is always so quiet and hard to read, hearing his point of view was surprising because we never knew anyone supported us or thought it was a great idea. He has always helped where he could, taking in letters or parcels for us and shipping bank cards, etc. when they have expired. One time we ordered a load of parcels from eBay, about 25 parcels came in over the week, and David's Dad was on a first name basis with the postman. Thank you. x

What did you think when you first heard our plans?

I was half worried about the education for the children, but also happy that you were going abroad everywhere, where I would have perhaps liked to have gone. I think the biggest concern was the children's education, and perhaps their welfare if you weren't sure where you were going to be living from one week to the next. Other than that, I thought it was quite a good idea.

The children might not be getting history lessons and a lot of the things that they are doing in schools. But they are getting to learn more about life and other people, which I think makes a lot more sense.

What were your thoughts when we in fact gave everything up and flew off?

When you said about it, I could tell straight away you were planning what you were going to do and how you were going to do it, rather than whether you were going to do it. I did wonder whether you realised perhaps how hard it was going to be, or whether it wasn't as hard as I think it would have been. And I suppose another thought I had was the language problems.

What are your thoughts now, six years later?

Well, most of the time, you've got a great life. You've explored a lot of the world. There's a lot more to see, I suppose, and there's a lot that you have done that I think I am a bit envious of.

The children's education seems to have gone okay. I haven't tested them or anything. A lot of things that I was taught in school when I was there have changed, you've got a machine to

do it for you now in your pocket. Or you don't even need it. Like algebra, they tried to teach me algebra. I couldn't do algebra and I have never found any time that I have ever needed it.

They're learning to get along with different people from different backgrounds and cultures and so forth. As the world is very mixed, being open-minded and talking to others will help them greatly. Learning more how to find out things, rather than knowing things. That's what one of my teachers told me once, "I could never teach you everything, but I can teach you how to find it out." He wanted me to know where to look for the answers. I suppose there's Google and everything, where you can do that nowadays. I've got a load of books in the front room that I can do the same. Knowing where to find the answer is far more useful than memorising a bunch of dates or figures.

They can read and write, in more than just their own language. Being with different people from different countries, mixing with everyone. They pronounce somethings differently. They write somethings differently. But if you can read and write and do math. You do use math to a certain extent. You don't need algebra so much. But basic math, you use every day. You go shopping, you've got to know how much something's going to cost, and how much change you should have. And you have the currency exchanges to work out on top of that and your children do that well.

Where do you see the children ten years from now?

It's hard to say. I don't even know where I'd be in ten years' time.

I don't know, especially with Tegan, the way is hers to create.

Whereas Tyler could become the new David Attenborough, with his passion for nature and wildlife.

There are some people that go and study in books for years and years but don't know anything when they have completed their studies. Others, like with building, Steven (my Uncle) has never done any building qualifications, not to my knowledge. But he can build a house, and he knows which way to put what in.

Whether to put the floor in before you do the walls, or whether you put the wall in first. He knows which way everything goes.

He didn't pass any building exams or anything, he just picked it up over years. He'll probably tell you more about it than somebody who's got all the exams and everything. That's how I see Tyler doing it.

What would stop you from doing this lifestyle?

My biggest problem would be finding work. Where will you find work and a house? You're all right because you're on the internet doing most of your work by computer.

You can do yours anywhere. Whereas let's say I was a driver. I might not get a driving job in Spain quite so easy or anywhere else like that. That'd be the hardest part, to get the job where you get the house. And if you move three months later, finding it again. You just about to get promoted and then you're moving on again.

DEREK HERBERT – David's Dad

Mark is a dear friend, a truly genuine guy. We met him at a Fearless Speaking event that we attended back in 2015 and have stayed close friends ever since. He had an eye-to-eye connection with David and that was when the pair of them truly opened up to each other. Mark has seen the children flourish over the years and supports us with his kind words.

What did you think when you first heard our plans?

Personally, I thought, wow, amazing, I'd love to do that. Travel around the world and get actual, real-life skills and actually understand and learn about the world's source energy. It can't be written. It's amazing. That's what I thought. Wow.

What were your thoughts when we in fact gave everything up and flew off?

I thought to myself, it's amazing. I take my hat off to you guys. I would love to have done it, but I am scared to do it. My wife would never do that because she likes structure. I think that everybody's got that hidden journey, to go out and take that adventure. We will all sit behind and judge it while somebody else is doing it, when we secretly inside would love to do it ourselves.

What are your thoughts now, six years later?

Another wow. The growth is unbelievable. The knowledge is amazing. The skills that all of you have learnt throughout the journey can only be learnt through the experiencing of you taking action, of actually doing instead of reading about it in books. Because transformation comes only from the doing, not from gaining the information.

Where do you see the children ten years from now?

They'd be living their dream and not following anybody else's dream. They'd be doing their thing for them because they're learning about themselves. Just because they're born in England, doesn't mean that they have to stay in England. They'd be aware of that. They'll be living, they'll be doing what they want to do. If they want to marry somebody from a different culture, different country, they'll do that. If they want to live in the mountains and live with sheep and herd goats and things like that, they'll do that. They'll have that experience of choice. They'll have the beauty of known creation. I see them following their dreams, whatever works for them, not actually following in society's dreams.

They will be happy in whatever they're doing because they're blessed to have parents like you guys. Because you guys took action. They always say, the smartest and the wisest children are the children who have travelled because they know a different way to live, and of life.

What would stop you from doing this lifestyle?

I think the fear that would hold me back, which didn't hold you guys back, I was trying to please everybody else. The fear of the unknown, the fear of stopping creation dead in its tracks.

That's what holds me back, because I don't know the unknown. If I was with somebody who said to me, let's go on this journey together, let's see what happens, let's rent out our house, let's just go and travel the world and see where the world takes us and see what we can learn in the world... What an adventure. Wow. I'd love to do it. I'd do it tomorrow.

What stops most people is their own judgement of what they think would happen. They're only coming from a place of love, and they're only coming from a place of not knowing, and they're only trying to fit into what they class as normal. They just don't know. And if they don't know, can we judge them for the unknowing? I think really and truly, people do things because they really love you, they really care. It's either coming from a place of hurt or love.

Really and truly, who would not love to have your adventure? To go out and just go and do whatever you want to do, and just see what you can create while you are out there doing it. If you never had fear inside you. everyone would do it. Why do people go on holiday? Because they want to create something different to what they're used to. They can handle it short term. But the thing is that, if you are creating something long term, then there's always more benefits than in short term.

I am so proud of you guys.

MARK HARRIS – Family Friend

Louise is a beautiful lady. We met her at the Fearless Speaking events and got to know her very well. She taught Tegan how to speak at her best. Louise lives in London and was the first place we stayed in London. Helping us to switch places from Cornwall to London, giving us that breathing space that we needed to start saving / repaying a little money. She got to know our kids first-hand (sorry about the chicken) and to see how they have grown today into thriving kids. Louise was our greatest friend and support in the first few crazy months, her friendship and kindness meant everything to us. We are forever grateful to you Louise.

What did you think when you first heard our plans?

Wow, that's brave, especially with young children and not knowing what the next stop is. How will they survive?

What were your thoughts when we in fact gave everything up and flew off?

Initial thoughts were, wow, they are actually doing this, followed by good luck. I look forward to seeing the photos.

What are your thoughts now, six years later?

I can't believe it's six years... it seems like only the last two years or so. It just shows when you have a mission / goal you can really make whatever you want work out and no doubt it gets easier in time and the children are older now, so it makes things even nicer as they grow into this lifestyle and not know anything other.

Where do you see the children ten years from now?

In 10 years, Tegan will be 23. Blimey that's scary. She will be well into her own flow and business by then. May have even settled somewhere herself and doing her own thing. Tyler I can imagine will be taking his time using all the technology available to invent cool things to help save the animals and planet.

What would stop you from doing this lifestyle?

I have to admit I'm a homing bird and even the thought of not knowing where my next income or stop would be is a bit scary. I think I'm settled now doing what I love here.

LOUISE MCNESTRIE – Family Friend

As you have seen, there are many takes on our life choices, and there are *some* who still think we are crazy, and it's those who are closest to us. Remember the "Box Story" at the beginning? Some people will always live in their little box of comfort. Our close family and friends do not want to see us succeed any more than they want us to fail, they would rather we stay closely aligned with them. If we step out, grow and succeed, how do you think it will make them feel? Insignificant? Stuck? Fearful for us?

Do not let the thoughts of friends and family hold you back from being remarkable. As you grow, you will find a more aligned group of friends, who support your dreams and goals whole heartedly, and like us, family will support you when you succeed, so maybe you do not need to talk to them for a couple years while you go out there on your terms and smash it.

CONCLUSION.

Six years later, after doing all of this travel, was it worth it? We certainly had many lows, but our highs were the highest highs we have ever experienced. And we got to experience them together. Instead of trying to survive and just trying to make it through the next week, the next month, trying to survive day by day, we are now flourishing and thriving. Life has never been the same, because we dreamt big and we took action. Now it's your turn. After every chapter, we've included online activities to help you create your action to create your life by design, some ways for you to get clear on how you could do things differently, what changes you could make, and what strategies would work best for you and your family.

Start taking action. Start filling in those sheets, start talking to your partner. If you've got kids, get them involved too, and start pulling out some ideas. Go get a big world map and put it on your wall. Have everyone stick post-its on the places where they want to go and say why.

Start making these discussions happen. And remember, those who love us dearly, you know who I'm talking about, the mother-in-law, the aunts, the uncles, the great-grans, if they're living in the box, they will not see your vision. They will do all in their power to try and keep you neatly in the boxes that they know and *understand.* So they're not the ones to be discussing this with. Go find those like-minded people. Come join our community, and get involved in the groups that you are interested in.

Take it one step at a time. We did go from a big house to carry-on suitcases and world travel, but that did not happen overnight. It took preparation. It took planning. It took self-growth and self-development. We've learnt and grown more than ever in these last six years. It has enabled us to step up and be the best humans we can be, to be the best partners we can be and to be the best parents we can be, and live the best example to others that we can be.

We're hoping that our journey, our craziness, our adventurous spirits, and our out-of-the-box thinking is so out there that it will give you permission and that self-belief that you too can make a difference. You too can make a change and step out and do what you know is best for you and your family.

When would NOW be a good time to start implementing and taking action?

When you have filled out those cheat sheets, go through them together with your partner or kids. If you want feedback, connect with us, share with us, share with our community about where you are and what it is that's holding you back. Join us at one of our online or in-person events and retreats and break out of the mould, get out of those boxes for a few days. Come join us and our amazing adventurous family and see how life can be so different, so unique, so brilliant. Come learn how you can create your life, your way. Your life by design.

You can check out *Your Action Plan* here.

Using all you have unlocked and discovered, it is time to put it all together to create your plan of action, to create your life by design.

Activities.foreverfamilyforeverfree.com/destiny

RESOURCES

GETTING US STARTED
TONY ROBBINS UPW - https://www.upwvirtual.com
NETWORK BIZ - https://networkcentral.biz
KNOW YOUR NUMBERS - https://www.foreverfamilyforeverfree.com/know-your-numbers
RICH DAD POOR DAD AUDIO BOOK - https://youtu.be/gliZHyovl7c

MAKING MONEY ONLINE
4 HOUR WORK WEEK - https://fourhourworkweek.com
AMAZON AFFILIATE - https://affiliate-program.amazon.co.uk
FOREVER LIVING - https://joinnow.foreverliving.com
HERBALIFE - https://www.herbalife.co.uk/business-opportunity
BOOKS BOOST BUSINESS $2,000 COMMISIONS - https://affiliates.booksboostbusiness.com
FIVERR - https://www.fiverr.com/start_selling
ONLINE JOBS - https://uk.indeed.com/Online-jobs
https://www.jobsite.co.uk/jobs/part-time/online

TRAVEL GADGETS
Apark-Universal-Adapter-Worldwide-Converter
Cities-Cabin-Approved-Trolley-21-Inch
Extension-Strips-Outlets-Protection-Braided

HEALTH & HYGINE
https://shopnow.foreverliving.com/gbr/en-gb/products/personal-care/028-FOREVER-BRIGHT-TOOTHGEL
https://shopnow.foreverliving.com/gbr/en-gb/products/personal-care/633-ALOE-LIQUID-SOAP
https://shopnow.foreverliving.com/gbr/en-gb/products/022-ALOE-LIPS-WITH-JOJOBA

COST OF LIVING
https://www.worlddata.info/cost-of-living
https://www.numbeo.com/cost-of-living

FLIGHTS
RYAINAIR PRIORITY –
https://help.ryanair.com/hc/en-gb/articles/360017825358-Priority-2-Cabin-Bags
SKYSCANNER https://www.skyscanner.net
KAYAK - https://www.kayak.co.uk
NORD VPN - https://nordvpn.com
WHAT FOOD CAN YOU TAKE ABOARD -
https://www.travelandleisure.com/food-drink/souvenir-foods-you-can-and-can-not-take-through-tsa
AIRLINE SIZE RESTRICTIONS - https://upgradedpoints.com/travel/airlines/carry-on-luggage-size-chart

Resources

CARS
CAR HIRE EXCESS INSURANCE - https://www.reducemyexcess.co.uk
WEBUYANYCAR - https://www.webuyanycar.com

STORAGE
DASH STORAGE - https://www.dashselfstore.co.uk

THRIFT STORE
UTAH AND LA - https://www.deseretindustries.org

PLACES TO STAY
AIRBNB - https://airbnb.co.uk   https://airbnb.com
PREMIERE INN (mid-range hotel chain) - https://www.premierinn.com
https://www.couchsurfing.com
https://homelink.org/en - (we haven't used these)
https://www.caravanclub.co.uk – (we haven't used these)

HOUSE SITTING SITES
https://www.nomador.com
https://www.mindmyhouse.com
https://www.housesittersuk.co.uk

HOMESCHOOLING ONLINE CLASSES
https://www.gov.uk/home-education
https://uk.ixl.com
https://www.abcmouse.com
https://www.adaptedmind.com
https://readingeggs.co.uk
https://www.muzzybbc.co.uk
https://www.duolingo.com/
https://www.facebook.com/groups/the2poundtuitionhubhomeeds

HOMESCHOOLING FACEBOOK GROUPS
Worldschooling Brits - https://www.facebook.com/groups/214314972339014
Worldschoolers Europe 2018 And Beyond -
https://www.facebook.com/groups/2022676397964692 -
Worldschoolers Explore the USA - https://www.facebook.com/groups/1842724762611474
Nomadic Network - https://www.facebook.com/groups/nomadicnetwork
World schoolers Nomads - https://www.facebook.com/groups/WorldschoolersNomads

OUR COMMUNITY GROUP
FOREVER FAMILY FOREVER FREE –

https://www.facebook.com/foreverfamilyforeverfree
https://www.youtube.com/foreverfamilyforeverfree
https://www.instagram.com/foreverfamilyforeverfree
laurahelen@foreverfamilyforeverfree.com

ATTENTION:Dreamers, Conscious Parents, Explorers and Families Seeking Freedom...

New Program Shows 21 Virtually UNKNOWN Secrets To Create Freedom And Start Travelling NOW!

So... What Are These 21 Travel Secrets (And How You Can Use It To Start Your Journey!?!)

Over the past five years we have supported many individual's, couples and families to figure out which of our travel strategies work best for them? Our different strategies work for almost every situation you can dream of.

If your goal is to visit different countries on a budget, we have travel hacks for that...

If your goal is explore new places, cultures and languages, we have travel hacks for that as well...

Week #1: How To Create Your Families Plan

Week #2: Discover Your True Potential

Week #3: Schooling Your Kids

Week #4: Working Remotely

Week #5: How To Get Travel Ready

Week #6: How To Travel Far On A Budget

www.foreverfamilyforeverfree.com/life-by-design

NOTES

NOTES

FOREVER FAMILY
FOREVER FREE

Printed in Great Britain
by Amazon

83539559R00099